A Strategy for Education

A Strategy for Education

Herman T. Epstein

⤨

New York OXFORD UNIVERSITY PRESS 1970

Preface

My activities in educational research were stimulated very much by the fact that my oldest child was approaching college age. I have had experience enough with education at that level to know that I didn't want my children to have such a depressing educational experience as I felt was common to virtually all institutions of higher education in the United States.

I first worked on a high school science curriculum project to get an idea of the best that was being done in curriculum development. My independent research activities began with development of a biology course for non-science students, and evolved from that when it became apparent that this first experiment had succeeded for reasons whose implications went far beyond my initial intentions and insights. Three years later I am still working on ramifications of that first set of results.

The pressure to produce a detailed description of these activities and ideas arose as a result of an interview by a reporter from *Time* Magazine. His article appeared and, as forecast by the reporter, brought forth a minor flood of inquiries and invitations to consult and to give talks. After many dozens of talks it became clear that something would have to be written, for two reasons. First, I do not have the talents which permit an actor to play his role for several years without going stale. I became bored and, occasionally, exasperated with people who asked me to explain my activities. Second, now that the method has been tried successfully in a dozen universities in three countries and in six different subjects, the system is going out of my control. I have therefore tried to give a detailed account of what I think I understand about my educational activities so that those who try the method elsewhere can know what is really involved. Then, when their experiments fail, as some likely will, they may be able to discover the sources of the failure so that we can learn from them.

It has been both humbling and gratifying to make a list of those whose help I want to acknowledge. However, to the students with whom we worked there goes little special commendation; frankly, they had little to lose.

Professor Maurice Sussman was the first colleague to volunteer, and his contagious enthusiasm brought in Professors Lawrence Grossman and Raymond Stephens. The summer program for the Thirteen College Curriculum Development Project was designed and executed with the superb and committed help of three other Brandeis colleagues: Professors Attila O. Klein, Herbert Oberlander, and Edgar Zwilling. The cooperation of the supervising staff of that program was due mainly to Professors Paul Brown, Fred Humphries, and Conrad Snowden. I am deeply grateful to the thirteen biology professors for their willingness to expose their areas of ignorance to each other and to me. It takes profound dedication to the cause of teaching young people to permit such public tampering with individual senses of dignity. The economics trials were done by Professors Harold Goldstein at Northeastern University and Richard Weckstein at Brandeis University. Professor Amos De Shalit made the arrangements and found the support for the experimental adult education course given in Rehovot, Israel, during my visit in the spring of 1969. His premature death in the fall of 1969 was a great blow to education as well as to me, personally. Professor Eugene Rosenberg conducted the U.C.L.A. trial with his characteristic enthusiasm and thoroughness which resulted in the rapid growth of use of the method at his university. Professor Kenneth Bott of the University of Chicago was the key man in the successful experiment at that institution. And, this book would not now be appearing without the thoughtful insights and help of Professor Arthur Peacocke of Oxford University.

I still don't know whether to thank or curse our director of public relations, Mr. Richard Gilman; it was he who contacted *Time* Magazine with the result that my life has been pressured ever since September 1968.

My debts to my parents are quite specific. To my father I owe the belief that I could do something of value in the intellectual world. To my mother I owe whatever feeling I have for people that makes me want to help them. This book is dedicated to their memory.

Finally, I am pleased to thank the Guggenheim Foundation for the award which helped give me the leisure to undertake the writing.

H.T.E.

Tel Aviv

May 1970

Contents

A Strategy for Education

Introduction

The number of students dropping out of college before finishing is estimated to be nearing half of those entering. The dimensions of this failure of our colleges are so great that it is amazing that the rebellions in colleges did not begin before the 1960's. Since a similar fraction of students fails to finish high school, it will not be surprising if rebellions begin there in the 1970's.

These rebellions have been ascribed to a complex of many factors: war, politics, poverty, affluence, psychology, society, and inadequate educational structures. Those who stress educational factors have paid little attention to the college level, yet the failure rate in colleges is indicative of a more serious educational problem there inasmuch as only the most capable of youths enter colleges. How is it possible that these bright youngsters can fail to find challenges and satisfaction in their studies?

As a result of the orientation to psychological explanations in our society, critics have tended to focus on the role of the students in the failures, with notable exceptions such as John Holt, whose book *How Children Fail* really deals primarily with how the schools fail the children. It is time that the focus shifts to the colleges themselves and to their instructional methods. If present-day colleges are so boring to so many of our brightest students, what is to be expected as the proportion of college-attending youth increases? The relationship between school and society needs desperately to be examined and re-examined because it is a major problem of our time. For lack of serious attention to that relationship, the main focus has been on development of new educational programs.

Before 1956, educational developments in the United States were almost completely in the hands of educators working in graduate schools of education. The advent of Sputnik brought about a thorough re-examination of the content of high school science courses beginning with the project of the Physical Science Study Committee. These new projects, which looked afresh at the contents of courses, have been organized and led very largely by professional scientists who gave up part of their university activities to accept the long-neglected responsibility of university scholars for what is taught in high schools. High school teachers and professors of education have also made an important contribution to all these projects. More recently, the reworking of high school curricula has been extended to non-science subjects. There have been conferences on education in such prestigious places as the White House in Washington and at Woods Hole.

The 1959 Woods Hole Conference on Education has been summarized and analyzed in Jerome S. Bruner's book *The Process of Education*. It seemed to be generally felt, judging from reviews of the book, that the conference was a milestone in education in the United States. But, in rereading Bruner's account, I have been struck by the fact that the educational aims and insights discussed therein are still those offered by educational thinkers beginning at least as far back as Plato. The advances made by that conference seemed to lie in its assembling substantial empirical support of the practicable nature of some of those aims which had previously had only the support of the reputations of the philosophers and educational theorists who had developed them.

The educational activities of the Sputnik era have thus been numerous and of high quality. Yet, to take the most striking example, statisticians tell us that enrollments in high school physics have declined steadily during that era. By the enrollment criterion, then, the various physics projects have been failures. The technical advances made by these projects in developing high school physics curricula are obvious to anyone with even a little background in the physical sciences. Yet, since these new courses have failed to attract more students to the study of physics, the failure must lie in *non-curriculum aspects* of the school and college situations. Great lip service has been payed to some of these, including the strategies and methods of instruction, but virtually nothing has been done. At first thought, it would appear harder to achieve progress in those aspects than in curriculum because this depends more directly on the increased effectiveness of what is at one and the same time the weakest link and the most important factor in teaching: the teacher. Projects to improve the curriculum have had to devote as much time to teacher training and retraining as to the curriculum itself. How much harder it should be to focus the hope for improvement on getting teachers to change their methods and strategies in the classroom!

Yet, since so much depends on the teacher, it is likely that methods for achieving substantial progress in education should come mainly from experiments at two extremes of the teacher problem: changing the teacher's methods and eliminating the teacher. The latter extreme is undergoing substantial trial in the form of television program teaching, programmed learning projects, and computer-assisted education developments. As results begin to pile up in the 1970's, we will acquire useful information about the extent to which the jobs of teachers can be made "less impossible" by giving them technological aids.

It is the other extreme—restructuring teaching methods—that has received less attention recently. This is true for several reasons, among which the two most important are, I believe: (1) the fact that it is very hard to imagine new methods; and (2) the fact that the only way to find and try new methods is to try them out yourself. The pre-Sputnik developments worked out at colleges of education were aimed at new methods for teachers. Their successes were minimized by the fact that few workers had the opportunity to be themselves involved in testing the new curricula, with the exceptions of some high school teachers co-opted on to such projects finding the time and energy to work on both projects and project trials. It is much easier to work out the details of what someone else has to do, as I know from my own experience with one of these projects.

As student demand for a change in the Biology course for non-scientists at Brandeis increased, it was necessary to examine what was being done by those colleagues who had been in charge of the course for some years. Examination revealed that they were doing a good job, that the course content was up-to-date and well organized, and that the instructors were keenly interested in doing their job. It is not that their course (or the similar course at other colleges) couldn't stand substantial improvement. Indeed, one of the biggest improvements that can be made easily in such courses is simply to change teachers to relieve the tiredness that afflicts every course taught by one person year after year.

After lengthy consideration of the goals and tactics of such courses, a new goal and a new set of tactics were devised and a new course was given. The apparent success of the course was so obvious that we began to wonder how it was that much more was achieved than had been intended. Analysis of the new course and of students' comments indicated that the new strategy appeared to have reopened the students' stores of curiosity about how science is done. This reawakening of curiosity is an important event and has even more important implications for our understanding of the processes of learning and teaching.

It is the purpose of this book to give an account of the new course and the implications derived from it. The account is entirely in the tradition of the experimental scientist in that the experiments will be presented first as thoroughly as possible. Only then will substantial interpretive remarks be made. These remarks are accompanied by references (in brackets) to Appendix 3 which includes quotations related to the topic discussed in the text. These quotations are from evaluation sheets turned in by students who were in the course during the academic year 1968–69. They are meant to show that the students' experiences had independently led them to the same inferences as those drawn by their instructors.

CHAPTER II

The Background of the First
of the New Courses

In the United States there are currently three main kinds of courses in science for non-scientists. First there is the science course for scientists. This is given to non-scientists on the grounds that anything less is an inadequate presentation. How can we believe for a moment that a watered-down course can give the student an idea of what the science is really all about? The dignity and integrity of the science must be preserved if the non-scientists are really to gain an appreciation of what science is all about.

Second is the survey course, which usually is a more episodic presentation of the major concepts and insights of the science. The argument here might be that we are not trying to train scientists and it is therefore better for the non-scientists to get an over-all view of science's accomplishments than to acquire the detailed knowledge that is expected of the budding professional scientists. Furthermore, the introductory course for scientists omits many or even most of the major accomplishments and ideas because these will be presented in later courses. The more important of these should be made known to the non-scientists who, after all, are likely to be taking their last course in a particular science. Thus, the first course for scientists is not at all appropriate for those desiring an over-all presentation of a particular science.

The third kind of course is derived from the post-World War II educational thinking of Harvard president James B. Conant. He devised what he called the case study method. This name is not at all what is meant as used, for example, by faculties of law and business. The latter present an actual case as it arose. The students go through the reasoning and activities of the professionals who handled the actual case; students thereby begin to learn the nature and scope of the professional activities expected of them. Conant's method gives a combined historical and conceptual development of some of the great insights in science. For example, one such topic is the development of the idea of the atom and the molecule. Conant's method selects out the experiments and speculations that eventually led to the postulation and subsequent proof of the existence of atoms and molecules.

It is possible to take issue with each of these three kinds of courses. The use of the science course presupposes that the usual introductory course is actually good for scientists. The survey course may well fall into the category of courses which offer non-scientists an over-all view of a field at which the students have no desire to look. And, the Conant method shows how some important concepts were evolved but gives the students little idea of what scientists actually do or what the scope of the science may be. Nevertheless, each type of course may well be suitable for some of the non-science students. If students were free to choose among these types, we could soon determine what the students themselves believe most desirable.

It is not possible to choose among the types on the basis that certain courses have a proportion of students who do excellent work. Almost any course by almost any teacher using almost any method and almost any textbook will have *some* excellent students. The fact is that there are some individuals whose turn of mind and intelligence will extract a great deal from any situation in which they are placed. Generalizations are usually made about the rest of the students: those whose activity, commitment, and effective working depend on factors external to themselves. Some teachers refer to these students as being without motivation and curiosity. Functionally, the reference is quite accurate; developmentally it is probably inaccurate. We all know how bright and filled with curiosity are most young children. We all know equally well that the brightness fades into dullness and the curiosity dries up so that such children seem uninterested in almost everything that is placed before them. For this reason, such people should be characterized as having their motivation and curiosity repressed by a combination of social, psychological, and educational factors. This is an important difference because it changes the task of later education and re-education from one of creating something where there was nothing (that is, motivation where there is only apathy) to a less difficult task of removing the repression of the motivation and curiosity.

In the United States only about one-third of people of college age attends college. Yet, these better-than-average youngsters receive the entire spectrum of grades from excellent to failure. How is it possible that a substantial fraction of our brightest young people fails courses in science designed for them? College teachers will disagree about the proportion, but they will agree that many college students are uninterested in studying any particular subject that they choose for themselves, let alone a required course in science for non-scientists. These young people have had experiences in school and in society which resulted in their being without much curiosity and motivation. And, since the science courses do not change the proportion of poorly performing students, it is clear that all three current types of courses are unsuccessful. No such course should be considered successful unless most of the top third of our youngsters achieve a good understanding of the subject, usually signified by an honor grade.

This assertion of lack of success of the three current types of courses can be seen to be supported by imagining another situation. Suppose that students were not required to study science. How many would then take science courses? We do not have to know the answer with accuracy to feel certain that most students would not take any science courses after the first one; they do not voluntarily take such courses now when they are required to expose themselves to some science in their first college year. If the courses were working well, one could expect some fraction of the students to take science courses without compulsion, but few colleges have enough confidence in their science courses to try the experiment by wiping out the requirements.

The upshot of the preceding remarks is that there is good reason to believe that our science courses do not succeed. Indeed, they may do positive harm by repelling and depressing students who might otherwise have found science exciting and inspiring. The fact that good students emerge from our courses may be blinding us to the possibility that better students might emerge in appreciably greater numbers from better courses.

The evaluation of newly developed high school and college science courses is still a subjective one, because there is no evidence that seems compelling to a substantial number of people. However, the very lack of clear-cut impressions of improvements is the first evidence that there has been little improvement due to these courses. One recent commentator, Prof. Robert S. Morison (Science *165*, 150–156, 1969), points to "the relative decline in students entering the sciences and the scientifically based professions," and comments that "elegant though the Physical Science Study Committee Physics Course undoubtedly is, it has not proved much more successful than any other method in making physics attractive to secondary school students."

It is unlikely that there is even a small fraction of scientists that does not believe that the above-mentioned PSSC physics course is far superior to its predecessors. Despite that evaluation, Morison's point is that little has been achieved by that excellent new course. It must therefore be recognized that the curriculum or content of such courses is not the aspect most in need of improvement.

With this insight into what is crucially important in design of science courses, it is possible to assert that all three types of courses for non-scientists are stressing the wrong factors, because all emphasize the content or the information about science and its development. The assertion does not help much in finding a new emphasis. Yet it is not difficult to arrive at a new emphasis if one asks what one would want to know about the fields of his own colleagues. My own outlook has always prompted me to ask, say, an economist friend what he really does when he's working. What is a problem for him? How does he tackle his problems? Why does he tackle them that way? Once I know the answers to these kinds of questions, I can hope to understand economists and their activities on any economic question, given a little help with its factual background.

In our case, we want to design a course to teach what a biologist does when he's doing his biology. If the student can learn an answer to this question for any one biological problem, it should not be hard to explain biology in general, because the essentials of particular problems differ little from one field of life to another.

This is close to what Bruner has in mind when he writes about understanding the structure of a science. In his book, *The Process of Education,* he presents four themes emerging from the 1959 Woods Hole Conference on Education. These are, briefly (1) the role of structure of a subject; (2) the readiness for learning; (3) the nature of intuition; and (4) stimulation of the desire to learn. Theme number one can be summarized by asserting that the purpose of education is to give students an understanding of the fundamental structure of whatever subject we teach in order to make their thinking fully effective. It is not education's main purpose to convey facts and techniques and theories. And, further, Bruner goes on to note that very little is known about how to teach this structure.

The reason it is not known how to teach the structure may well be because we do not yet know what the word really means. Indeed, the stress on theme three may well derive from the fact that we are still groping for a clear statement of what the structure of a subject really is. Yet, it is possible for Bruner to state that research in learning has shown definitively that knowledge acquired without sufficient structure to tie it together is knowledge likely to be forgotten. And, when he writes such a statement, we know, intuitively, what is meant.

To develop the new method we have proceeded in an essentially empirical way. We can tell you what to do but not, on any fundamental level, why to do it that way. The result is a sort of cook book set of homely maxims about how to teach what has come to be called the research studies method. Naturally, there were speculative reasons for the particular tactics that were developed, and these will be stated as clearly as possible. However, they must be taken only as heuristic.

How does one go about conveying what a biologist does when he is doing biology? The most direct way is to have the student do biological research in the laboratory. This, however, is not generally feasible because it simply takes too long to acquire the skills and understanding of techniques needed in current science research. It is true that the students could profit by using time in this way, so that the direct method should be used whenever the teaching time is available. But, generally, there is not enough teaching time. And, it is by no means obvious that the bulk of the students can be interested enough in what is done in a laboratory to keep them at the work until the fruits of the labors become manifest enough to provide the motivation for continuing. Parenthetically, I would like to plead that someone should take the time and trouble to try this method.

The next most direct way is to have the student go through the intellectual processes and experimental details as they were experienced by a scientist in doing his research. There are two clear alternative ways of going through this material. The simple way would be to tell the students about it as a sort of continued story for, say, an hour three times per week. Even though the method is clear and easy to do, intuition told me that the students would not really care. In fact, it seemed to me that this was a prime instance of conveying to students much more than they care to know about a subject they would not care to master.

The other alternative seemed more plausible as a method. This is to have the students themselves re-create the research: to let them read through a set of research papers. The set would have to be chosen carefully, and would have to be studied with help from the instructor. The help would have to come in some special way, because otherwise the instructor would end up telling them the story himself, as in the first alternative. Having reached this conclusion, it nevertheless seemed to be preposterous. It amounted to conducting a graduate research seminar for 17-year-old students with little background and virtually no interest in science. The decision to attempt this method derived from thinking about an entirely separate aspect of American college education.

This separate aspect is that in research universities (which comprise perhaps 10 per cent of the colleges in the United States) the active research scientist does very little teaching, at least at the undergraduate level. Roughly, the situation developed because of what was a steadily increasing supply of research funds from the United States government. These funds permitted scientists to work at a pace unprecedented in history. Because some scientists could work at this pace, all were forced to adopt it because the alternative was their exclusion from the most significant and most tantalizing of current research problems. Those who could work, figuratively, 24 hours per day would simply finish each interesting problem before the more leisurely academic research scientists could mobilize their students and their laboratories. As a result, research scientists tended to teach only one course each term, and that was usually for graduate students and advanced undergraduate students. When there is only a limited time for teaching, one's primary obligation appears to be to the young science students who will succeed one's self in the profession.

This flight of front-rank research people from teaching undergraduates and especially first-year students is one which is not faced squarely by the universities, and, in my judgment, constitutes a major scandal whose origin is the lack of a sense of responsibility on the part of the faculties of research universities. For this reason, in rethinking the science course for non-scientists, I wanted to find a course which would reverse the flight from teaching. Rather than doing this by meeting the problem head-on, I tried first to analyze the situation to determine if a way could be found to induce these research scientists to *volunteer* to return to the teaching of first-year students in general and first-year non-science students in particular.

There seemed to be two criteria which needed to be satisfied if the scientists were to be persuaded to return to teaching at this level. The course should take virtually no preparation time and should be entirely fascinating to the scientists from the point of view of content. If such a course could be designed, it seemed to me that many colleagues would be tempted to return to teaching at that level. Even though the first criterion seemed to be an impossible one, analysis shows readily that both criteria actually describe the same thing: the scientist's own research field. For, no matter what aspect of his field had to be presented, the scientist could be presumed to have the important and the unimportant features at his fingertips. Further, scientists are usually quite free to choose their own lines of research. They therefore work on problems which most fascinate them. Thus, we are back to the starting point: the thing to teach is one's own research field, and the opportunity to do that should begin to induce a reversal of the flight from teaching first-year students.

The reversal of the flight from teaching is not simply a matter of getting academic scientists to assume their responsibilities as professional teachers. It is even more a matter of the success of a new approach to teaching. This follows because it is largely irrelevant if one person, such as myself, could carry out the development of any new course successfully without having made provision for the involvement of other teachers. Without the hypothetical inducements to my colleagues to become involved in the new course, it would not have been worth the bother to attempt its development.

It was then clear that there would be as many different courses as different instructors, so that the aims of such a course could not include any extensive common body of information. Nevertheless, one should hope for some things in common inasmuch as biology is structured along similar lines regardless of the particular organism and particular problems being studied. The way to achieve this common background was simply to use the papers being studied as points of departure to indicate to the students some of the generalizations and insights underlying their particular study. For example, if one studies photosynthetic organisms, it is necessary to indicate that photosynthesis is an alternative way for an organism to obtain the energy for making complicated molecules needed for both food and structure. Then, the digression would explain the energy mechanisms for organisms which are not photosynthetic, both because these mechanisms also exist in photosynthetic organisms and to reveal some of the variety of strategies by which nature obtains energy.

This way of thinking about the details permitted the inference that digressions would constitute a major part of the activities of the course to be developed, and one of the empirical parameters of the course would be the fraction of the time to be spent on digressions in comparison with the time spent on the research paper itself. An interesting possibility arose in thinking about this problem, for there seemed to be an opening for using the well-known finding of psychology that one picks up related information very rapidly and firmly if one is trying to understand a main set of points. This is an aspect of the remark by Bruner referred to earlier in which he asserted that knowledge acquired without sufficient structure to tie it together is knowledge likely to be forgotten. The positive statement of this remark is that knowledge acquired with other knowledge of importance to the individual is very likely to remain with him because it is tied up with the memory of important information. These tactics seemed to raise the very interesting possibility of a course containing *only* related information, provided the digressions were carefully selected so as not to depart very far from the main line of the class study activities. This constraint on digressions is another point to be studied empirically and constitutes one of what are now called the technical aspects of the teaching method.

Another technical problem was the permissible gap between successive papers. Since the students could not be expected to know much biology, it follows that very much time would be spent on the first paper in order to build up a background of information about the organisms, methods, and problems set forth in that paper. Presumably the second paper would require much less of the background-building, but the technical question concerned just how much new material could be in the second paper without leaving the students discouraged by the seemingly endless number of new concepts and methods to be learned. Somehow, the papers must be chosen so as to converge in such a way that the last few papers contained hardly more novelties for the students than they did for professional scientists reading them when they appeared. Still another technical question concerned how long to stay with any one paper. Clearly, it would take months to make the students sufficiently expert to appreciate all the aspects and details of a non-trivial paper. How can one decide when one has reached a point of diminishing returns? What does one do about the missing insights: those which are in the paper but which the class did not reach? I believe that this paragraph should make clear that there are, in fact, many technical questions. It should also be made clear that no attempt would be made to deduce the answers from any theory of teaching or of learning. Instead, variations would be made to determine empirically what worked well (and, with luck, best) when each of the technical parameters has been varied. Rather than make a catalogue of these technical questions and parameters, they will be discussed along with the description of the results, even though they were actually considered before embarking on the first trial of the course.

Finally, assuming the successful development of such a course, it appeared as though it could solve a very important recurrent problem in curriculum development. This is how to keep a curriculum up-to-date when science is moving onward so fast that textbooks go out-of-date within a few years of being written. In our method, every instructor will be teaching his own current field of interest. Therefore, as both fashions and insights of science evolve, the course topics, contents, and emphases will automatically change to keep up with the times. So, non-science students will always be studying problems of current interest using the most current concepts and experimental techniques. Therefore, there should be no need to consider large or fundamental changes in this course, once the format has been established.

CHAPTER III

The History of the First Course
and Its Consequences

The first trial of the new course took place in the second semester of 1967 with a class of twenty-five volunteers who agreed to leave the then regular two-semester biological science course for non-scientists. The volunteers were mainly first- and second-year students who were told nothing about the course other than that they would be reading original science research papers. The choice among volunteers was made on the basis of their grades to date; I selected five students each whose prior science grades were A, B, C, D, and E. There were about as many males as females.

The first paper was to be one entitled "Ultraviolet Inactivation and Photoreactivation of Chloroplast Development in *Euglena* Without Cell Death." This paper is only 1½ pages long. I have to admit that as I stood before the class on the first day and started to announce the first paper, my ability to speak vanished and I stood there frozen in panic. What, I asked myself, was I doing giving these uninterested and incompetent students a paper that would be entirely suitable for a graduate research seminar? I made the quick decision that it was all madness and that I would give them the paper to read but that during the first week I would figure out something less ridiculous to do. That decision unfroze me, and I was able to speak and ask the students to read the first paper for an hour or so and to return for the next class meeting with questions of all kinds, especially definitions of words and concepts. With that I launched into a discussion of how one chooses an object on which to work and pointed out that it was the biological problem that was of primary interest. Given a problem, biologists then tended to look for an organism in which the question could be most readily studied. The assertion was developed that social scientists do the same thing. The example used was the problem of the democratization of political power in republics. I did not have to know history or political science to get the class to realize that an historian with a background in United States history would study this problem by studying the Jacksonian era. Those with backgrounds in the history of other countries would study the problem at various other historical times. The point was made that this choice was based on the same kinds of selectivity criteria used by scientists.

If one chanced to know little about the most suitable organism, it might be that the study would proceed using the familiar one because the human cost of learning the new system might be greater than the extra effort involved in studying the problem in the less suitable but more familiar organism. (10,46) *

This particular first-day discussion has been used by me ever since because it involves an especially good question to raise with students since few seem to have thought about how scholars come to choose their problems. Most believe that one simply investigates in depth the organism or era or topic on which one has developed competence through previous acquaintance, generally at the time of working on a doctoral dissertation. It was, of course, necessary to admit that such a situation is actually true of many scholars and even, from time to time, of scholars who do occasionally manage to change organisms or eras or topics to suit the problem of interest. This first-day discussion has been presented to a number of those who later became associated with me

* Numbers in parentheses refer to student comments. See Appendix 3.

in teaching the new course, and some of them have adopted their own versions of this beginning.

The next class meeting produced a flood of dictionary-related questions. It was necessary to define the words ultraviolet, inactivation, photoreactivation, Euglena, cell, death, etc. Each definition naturally required an explanation, and the major problem was: just how superficial should each definition be? The rule I adopted has remained a useful one: if the concept can be explained in fairly simple experimental terms, it is done that way. If it would take too long to describe in terms of simple experiments, then it is explained superficially but with as little misinformation as possible.

It is probably self-evident that the explanation of any one term involved the use of other terms not understood by the students as a group. Therefore, the number of terms defined, explained, or made somewhat plausibly intelligible on the first day was about 30, although from the point of view of the student, we had actually defined only the few terms listed above. The second and third of the three one-hour classes per week followed roughly the same pattern of definitions and explanations, with strong emphasis on experimental definitions wherever possible.

As I pondered the events of the first week with a view toward deciding how to alter the course (as I had promised myself during the first moments of the first class meeting) it occurred to me that the students had gone through the definitions and explanations of perhaps 75 terms. This began to seem like a considerable accomplishment because most of the students appeared to have understood and perhaps even learned many or most of the terms in a situation in which the focus was on something else: obtaining the background to read and understand the paper. At this point, I realized for the first time that, in fact, some very substantial progress had been made. (33) For, to put the matter directly, what might have been the result if the students had been asked to learn the meanings of the 75 terms without having the research paper to support the learning? It seemed self-evident that this would have been a grand waste of time. Thus, this was a good illustration of the structured learning which, according to what I later found discussed by Bruner, has been found to be the only permanent way to learn anything. (23)

It was thus with some optimism that I decided to continue the course as originally developed for another week. During the second week, the students could begin to sketch the over-all purpose of the research, and even reached the point of outlining the detailed strategy of the first experiment described in the paper. During the third week we were able to set forth the raw data obtained, and show how to put them in a form suitable for analysis and interpretation. Finally, several alternative explanations for the data were found and the students began the scientists' standard procedure of reducing the number of alternative explanations by making predictions of what should be found in other situations. Their predictions were then compared with the results of related experiments, which I simply described to the class.

The class participation was surprisingly high, considering that many of the students were still recovering from the shock of being given such an assignment. Further, as students began to make some reasonable inferences from the data, an obvious heightening of interest resulted. At this point the class could be asked to propose the next experiments to be done. With help in deciding the kinds of approaches (physiology, genetics, microscopy, etc.) that existed, it was not difficult to get the class, as a whole, to propose three new studies, all of which were among the next papers prepared for them. This ability to make a step toward a new investigation seemed to me to raise the interest of several students, especially, of course, those who had proposed the next steps. (19)

The conduct of the class was mainly through questions, either from the students or from the instructor seeking to help the students formulate either answers or questions. This is perhaps best described as a dialectic exchange, differing from the Socratic in that the students lacked both information and analysis whereas Socratic dialogue is more strictly analysis of information already known. Two of the technical parameters were estimated during this first month: the frequency with which digressions could be started and the digression length. A rough rule was established that no more than three digressions should be made each hour and that no digression could last more than about five minutes; that is, the instructor should be careful to return the discussion directly to the paper every five minutes. Otherwise, the students appeared to lose a sense of direction and become restless because they were making no direct progress on their main objective: the understanding of the activity described in the paper.

At this point still another tactic was clarified. The attention of the class as a whole should continually be focussed on the actual activities (38)—including the strategy, tactics, and technical manipulations—of the authors of the research papers rather than on the information being obtained. Of course, it is not possible to exclude the emphasis on understanding the paper, but it became somehow evident that the students were pushing themselves to deeper thinking if there were continual reminders that they should be putting themselves in the place of the investigator in asking both what, precisely, is being done experimentally and what, precisely, should be done next. This is perhaps understandable if we remember that this verbal and reading approach is but a substitute for what would be more nearly an ideal course: a lengthy period of doing actual laboratory research. It was also the beginning of recognizing a corollary which must have considerable theoretical importance, probably more importance than the explanation of the tactic. That is, the student mind which is not captured by a recitation of the facts of science is nonetheless stimulated and involved by dealing with the actual research activities even in fields of interest far from his own. To say this directly, most students, in my experience, are not entranced by the three main types of courses set forth in the preceding chapter. But, their curiosity seemed to be reawakened by dealing with the actual activities needed for obtaining information. (8) This point will be taken up again in a later chapter in connection with inferences about experience-based learning.

The study of the second paper proceeded much like that of the first. To start with, terms were defined, concepts clarified, experimental techniques explained, and then we could work out the main objectives of the paper, the strategies, the actual tactics (the experimental approaches), the data, and the interpretation·of the data. During this period I found that, with some helpful hints, students could arrive at six interpretations for most non-trivial sets of experimental results. Frequently they offer many more interpretations, but a number prove, on examination, to be equivalent. This ability to find many alternative interpretations was, at first, very strange to students from the social sciences whose thinking tended to be one of either agreement or disagreement with the inferences of the authors of the papers. (35) Indeed, it had to be pointed out to them that the class had succeeded in finding six alternative explanations and that in the future we would always attempt to find that many alternatives, simply to show that it could be done. Emphasis on the development of alternative explanations of data yielded significant dividends in accelerating students' grasp of the idea that sciences advance by exclusion of alternative explanations and never by "proving" or supporting any given explanation. (47) It is easy to state the scientists' attitude, but the point is really brought home when the instructor can strike out explanations listed on a blackboard as the result of doing control experiments; the role of control experiments was made readily appreciated by having the list of alternative interpretations of the data on the blackboard.

This second paper took nearly 3 weeks to complete, so that we were now about halfway through the semester. It was only during this period that many of the students began to "catch on." The discussions sharpened appreciably, and students began to tell me how much they were enjoying some new-found aspects of thinking. Discussions began to include two-thirds of the students and the problem of class management appeared for the first time. This lag in "catching-on" has remained a constant feature of this course, although we have empirically found ways of shortening the lag period, as will be set forth in a later chapter.

Another question that arose during this second paper was the role of outside reading. It was not at all hard to keep the students from reading other materials during the first $1\frac{1}{2}$-page paper; there was too little material that was obviously related to anything of which the students had ever heard. For example, in talking about the effects of ultraviolet light, it became necessary to discuss briefly the physics of radiation, the chemistry of radiation, and finally the biology of radiation. There was no material on such topics in the books the students had read in high school. The second paper, however, referred to cytological features, and it was not at all surprising that students felt they could get something useful from reading in textbooks. However, some of the students later decided that there wasn't very much of use to them in textbooks since they couldn't get much from these books except general information. There are two explanations of this rather nebulous attitude. First, using terminology of psychology, students retain structured information, and the information in the textbooks generally wasn't directly related at all to the work being discussed. Second, textbooks try to teach something, whereas I was trying to help the students learn something. Perhaps teaching things, that is, giving lectures even to these seemingly quite mature and sophisticated students, was repressing their curiosity and motivation which were apparently being uncovered in my classroom. As will be discussed in a later chapter, both explanations appear to have considerable validity.

There was a puzzling differential student response to some of the digressions: great interest in some of the digressions and little in others. The difference didn't seem correlated with any "intrinsic" interest of the digressions. I decided, eventually, that it correlated with the sharpness and detail of my discussion. To say this directly and bluntly, if I knew very much about the subject, the students were very interested. If remarks were vague and general because I had little knowledge of more than textbook depth, student interest was low. (30) In a sense this is entirely to be expected, but the hand-waving kind of explanation had appealed to non-science students in my previous courses with them, so it seemed that in this class something new had been developed. These students who had previously been content with superficial and approximate explanations now wanted much sharper ones. This response is, in my mind, one that compels us to be much more critical of standard survey courses taught by one person. That person, with very few exceptions, has little more than textbook knowledge of many of the topics he discusses. If the students are accepting that kind of teaching, all is well. If however, students are being taken directly to the "real thing"—the original researches—they sense the sharp decrease of profundity of the instructor, and they react accordingly. This point can be summarized by J. Robert Oppenheimer's famous dictum: "you can't teach what you don't know."

The third and fourth papers took between one and two weeks each, and subsequent papers could be managed in one week each. An outstanding feature of the class as the course went on was the progressively greater involvement (both in number of students and in depth of questioning) of the students. (27) By this time it had appeared to me that all students except the very poorest were gaining appreciable insight into the nature of research in biology. In my estimation, some 80 per cent (36) of the students were involved in classroom discussions, and revealed an impressive growth in their ability to think analytically.

At least as impressive was the noticeable development of a problem-oriented attitude towards the topics. When a question arose, many students responded by talking aloud about what might be needed to solve the problem, whether genetics, physiology, cytology, or information from comparative biology or evolution.

Another feature that manifested itself during this second half of the semester was the surprisingly high interest in the details of experimental techniques. The remark of one of the students will illustrate the attitude. He said, "I used to think that scientists did miraculous things I could never understand. Now I know I can understand most of the miracles they do. And, you know, in spite of the fact that I understand them, they seem no less miraculous!"

By the end of the semester, it seemed self-evident that the course had succeeded in giving students an idea of what a biologist did when he was practicing his profession, and had done this in a way that was generally both interesting and stimulating to almost all of the students. (26) Indeed, there were many occasions on which I sensed that students were genuinely enthralled with both the science and their ability to understand it. Yet, there were obviously many factors that went into the apparent success of the course. One was the small class size which any student would prefer to the large and impersonal lecture. A second was the so-called "Hawthorne effect," which results in all changes being looked upon positively and reacted to with improved performances. A third was the very restricted amount of subject matter and required reading. A fourth was just the possibility that the learning was so superficial as to be merely titillating, with the result that the success merely reflected the easy way in which a very much disliked requirement could be fulfilled.

The problem of evaluation had not been faced at all. And so, at the last meeting of the class I could do no better than ask some colleagues to take over the class in my absence and find out what happened. Three biologists and a physicist accepted the responsibility. Their subsequent report can be summarized as follows. First, they were impressed with the extremely high level of student participation. The biologists began asking questions of a biological nature, and various students apparently were able to answer most of the questions in a reasonably satisfactory way. After about twenty minutes, several of the students became restless and interrupted to ask why the faculty people were there. My colleagues replied that they had come to try to ascertain what the students had gained from the experimental course. To this the students' rejoinder was, "Well, why don't you just ask us?" They were thereupon asked the question, and one of my colleagues summarized the generally agreed-upon reply in roughly the following terms. "We have learned that biology and probably science in general is a creative and respectable part of our culture. We used to think that scientists were like ditch-diggers whose activity was mainly a dull scraping away of the dirt covering dry factual bones. Now we know that scientists are creative intellectuals whose work is equally significant to what is done in the fields we hope to study ourselves." My colleagues reported one unsuspected finding. Most of the students had begun to wonder, late in the semester, if their ability to read scientific papers was due entirely to having studied a particularly trivial set of papers.

So, independently, many had gone to the science library and pulled from the shelves at random one or more of the journals. After some study, most seem to have convinced themselves that, apart from some missing factual background, they were capable of reading and understanding these randomly chosen articles. (41)

This last point underlines something that has been simply accepted up until now. These young non-science students had become very much at ease when faced with reading serious science research papers. They had studied eight such papers, and by the end of the semester they had acquired an impressive ability to read the papers and fashion a list of questions whose answers then permitted these students to understand at least the main points and usually the greater part of the paper. There was, of course, a gradation of abilities. (25) Indeed, as has been found also in later versions of this course, a fraction (perhaps 10–20 per cent) of the students maintained that they would have been happier with a conventional survey-type course. A very few students (1 or 2 out of 25) were so totally unable to understand the course that by any criterion they would have failed; in this first experimental course no one was actually failed.

The response to this trial was so encouraging that plans were made to try it again in the fall semester. Once it was known that such students could actually read science research papers, I could think of many new things to do that might improve the basic course appreciably.

During the summer, however, one colleague (who had followed the reports on the course very closely) came to ask if it were really true that this kind of course required virtually no preparation time. Again, I pointed out to him that he would be selecting a set of about ten papers in his own research area, and that it would be hard for him to justify spending more than ten minutes each day to think over the contents of one of these papers, especially since the earlier papers would take several weeks to cover in class. He finally convinced himself to try teaching a section (25 students) of what has come to be designated as "Biological Science 3a." This colleague is an extremely gifted lecturer and raconteur, as well as a stimulating and highly creative and productive scientist. He began talking about his projected participation in the course with such vigor that two other colleagues finally decided to join us, after the usual reassurances that there was virtually no preparation time once the papers had been selected. It is significant that one of these colleagues is from our graduate department of biochemistry which, as implied by the name, has no teaching responsibilities for undergraduates. Thus, this colleague was adding voluntarily an extra teaching responsibility. The involvement of these colleagues was, of course, the proof of the pudding: the research scientists could actually be induced to return to teaching first-year non-science students, given the opportunity to do so under the two criteria I had established for the new course.

During the following year, each instructor used papers from his own research field, and the results, subjectively, were entirely similar to those of the first trial course. One gratifying new problem appeared when about half of the students in each section requested a sequel course. For some of these students a sequel would have meant using up an elective course, as they had already fulfilled their science requirements. Since these students were our best ones, and since they were also among the brightest in their own areas of study, the request for a sequel can be taken as significant objective support for the claim that the new course was intellectually challenging and successful.

Inasmuch as my colleagues were repeating and testing the course design worked out from the first trial, it was possible for me to test various ideas suggested by the results of that first trial. The most important idea is one that is much discussed in educational circles today: the extent to which student response is enhanced by lowering the pressure on them to work. The application of pressure can be achieved by giving surprise quizzes —many quizzes—by urging students to study, by reacting negatively to their not being prepared, and by grading very severely. The result of using all these varieties of pressure was an appreciably less successful course; indeed, later student evaluation of the section confirmed most of the subjective impressions.

Later, in another section of this course, I used the same papers but applied virtually no pressure; the result was a class whose development had the same qualities as that of the first trial (8).

By the time all these sections of the course had been completed, various patterns had emerged. The over-all response in all sections was very high. The more the interest of the instructor was clearly exhibited (6), the more quickly the students responded by working hard without being pressured. All of the instructors "knew" without any objective evaluation that they had done something good and had probably enriched the lives of most of the students.

We also gained more confidence in the new method when it had been found to work with four different instructors using four vastly different subject matters. Indeed, in our later questioning of the students we were surprised to learn that many of the students who thought extremely highly of the course, nevertheless still had little interest in the particular topic. For example, some of my best students wanted to know why I insisted in using viruses as a topic when there were so many really interesting topics. (44)

With the assembly of insights from the four of us, it was possible to begin constructing a manual of suggestions for new instructors. We also agreed on a set of suggestions for students planning to enroll in the course. The necessity for both these steps was accelerated by the participation of the colleague from the graduate biochemistry department. At least six of his colleagues indicated that they would like to become involved in the course during the following year. It is worth recalling that members of that department are not expected to teach any undergraduates at any time. Thus, the expressed interest of these scientists was impressive evidence that the opportunity to teach under these new conditions was highly attractive, and that these apparently unconcerned research scientists really wanted to work with the students, including first-year non-science students. The flight from teaching appeared truly on the way to being reversed!

Our planning had to be carried further when the results of pre-registration for the following year became known. Nearly 200 returning students indicated that they wanted to enroll in this course during the next year. Since we could expect a similar number of entering first-year students, we were faced with providing sections for 400 students; at no more than 25 students per class, we needed 16 sections. We had only about 10 instructors available. After considering this problem for some weeks, we decided that we could safely try to use senior post-doctoral fellows —scientists who were at least one full year beyond the obtaining of their doctorates in science. The screening of potential instructors was mainly on the ability to feel comfortable when making up relatively superficial explanations for matters that could not be clarified on the basis of readily describable experiments. This aspect generally arose as the result of a question whose answer depended on knowing some factual material not yet covered in class. One should not get bogged down in the background details needed before the answer can be exhibited. (The rough rule of getting back to the research paper every five minutes had been changed to permit ten-minute digressions, but even this rule prevented lengthy background explanations.) Some instructors feel that it is deceptive and unwise to set forth partial or even partly inadequate factual information; such people should not attempt this new course. [There is no point in arguing about whether their attitude is correct. Some of us agree and others disagree with the activities, and there is no obvious way to decide such a question in a fashion that will be compelling to all instructors. Those who will not be able to teach in the rough fashion required by this new method should do what they do best. There are many courses to be taught, and it is better for each instructor to do what is most suited to his own nature.] With this criterion in mind, it was not difficult to assess potential new instructors. Anticipating the results of the following year's activities, it can be stated that the only relatively unsuccessful instructor was one who simply would not believe the recommendation concerning the pressure level in such courses. When he dropped the pressure late in the semester, the students responded as expected.

In the subsequent fall semester, there were 8 sections of the course, and 7 sections in the spring semester. Monthly meetings with present and past instructors permitted the evaluation of many ideas for improving the course and for solving various common problems that arose, as well as facilitating understanding of some of the established tactics. The results were again as successful as in the first year.

It should be noted that 14 of the 15 sections were taught voluntarily. That is, 14 instructors taught sections in addition to their normal activities of research and teaching, without teaching credit and without payment. It is not clear yet how the administration will handle the problem of recruiting and compensating this large number of volunteer instructors in the future. But, it is highly satisfying to have this problem rather than the one at the other extreme of the availability of instructors, which has been the situation prior to the introduction of this new course. The availability of the volunteers will apparently continue in the coming years so that, after just a two-year trial, it can be concluded that the problem of the biology course for non-scientists has a new solution. My department will continue to offer the more usual survey courses for non-scientists for those who prefer such courses and for those who cannot gain entrance into our course for lack of a sufficient number of instructors.

A problem of course management has appeared because of the large number of instructors. The monthly meeting appears to be the prime means of alerting new instructors and reminding veteran instructors of the strategies and tactics which are necessary parts of this method. However, there is no such possibility for meeting with those trying this method at other colleges. As a result, I have tried to discover and gather the results of all the stratagems that have been attempted at Brandeis University, and the inferences and suggestions form the contents of the next two chapters. The aim is to make available the combined experience and insight of some twenty instructors who have taught this method while in continual communication with each other. In addition, there are psychological inferences about the learning-teaching processes which seem empirically established by our combined experiences; these are presented in the way they appear to me.

The history of the first course would not be complete without some mention of its spread to other institutions. At the time of writing, the course had been tried, with apparent general success, in ten other universities in three countries (U.S.A., England, and Israel). The trial of the method at the University of California at Los Angeles deserves some special mention. During its first trial by a colleague and friend, four of his colleagues volunteered to teach sections, attracted by one or another of the features of the method. The subjectively assayed success was so great that during the next term, ten additional faculty people (all volunteers) joined the program and taught sections of the course. This experience entirely parallels that at Brandeis University in showing the ability of the method to reverse the flight from teaching. In addition, it gives substantial support to the speculative reasons for adopting the various stratagems we have developed during the testing at Brandeis.

CHAPTER IV

The Tactics of the Method

Discussions among the more than twenty instructors who have participated in this course have yielded a set of tactics which have been tested and retested so that it is possible for new instructors to learn what works and what doesn't work. Each new instructor can then adapt his own classroom personality to the experience-based framework for the method in a way that is suited to him. More important, there are special features of this approach which result in certain fixed demands on the instructors; if not adhered to, there is great likelihood that the course will become just another conventional science course for non-scientists, albeit with a rather novel course content.

A. THE ESSENTIAL FEATURES

First, the four most essential features will be presented, explained, and rationalized.

1. The class must be composed mainly of students just entering the university. In one sense, the whole method can be described as a graduate research seminar given for seventeen-year-old entering students with no background or interest in the subject.

2. The focus must be on the actual work done by an individual or group of individuals, not on the informational content of

the work. In this respect one distinguishes between studying a monograph on the origins of the Labour Party for (a) the traditional purpose of understanding its contents and (b) our purpose of trying to discover and understand how the author conceived, planned, and executed the obtaining of materials and the eventual writing of the monograph.

3. The class is conducted only through student questioning. There is virtually no lecturing as such, and the dialectic tone is maintained by the rough rule that instructors are not to be talking more than half the time.

4. There is no pressure exerted on the students to work or even to participate. We assert that the natural curiosity and motivation of students will eventually effect participation and even work on the part of students whose initial activities are restricted to physical presence in the classroom.

There have been students in this course who are at all stages of their university education; each has profited from the course and each has contributed according to his background. Yet, the fact that entering students can manage such a course leads to the conviction that they should be the preferred enrollees because of the effect on all their later studies. Even if the results of taking this course were confined to the students' attitude toward subsequent science courses it would be desirable as the first course, partly because it helps them in science courses but partly because it alters the "anti-science" attitude of many entering students and thereby broadens their horizons appreciably. This question of when students should take this course will arise again in connection with its use for serious students of science.

The focus on the tactical and manipulative *activities* of scientists is one whose emphasis has come from following the developments in all the various sections of the course. Without exception, every instructor who has not grasped this idea has discovered that the students eventually become bored with the papers. In almost every instance, the instructor has discovered for himself that the interest of the students can be reawakened by going to considerations of what the scientists actually do. If the focus is *not* on the activities of the scholars, it inevitably is on the informational content of the papers, and that interests only specialists and students who have already acquired a background in the subject.

A lecture is something that an instructor does to students, and will be successful only to the extent of student interest and competence in the subject. The purpose of our course is to help the students learn, and this can be achieved only by having them contribute most of the questioning and most of the discussion, with the instructor serving to supply two things: (1) factual information and (2) guidance toward an effective way of thinking about the subject. Ways of bringing about this high level of student activity will be considered later in this chapter.

The problem of pressure level in a classroom is not an easy one to discuss. The assertions in point 4 above are based on empirical findings to be presented in detail later. In particular there will be discussion of how to achieve student participation in discussions without exerting much of any pressure.

B. TACTICS FOR INSTRUCTORS

We now turn to the detailed tactics of the new course. The experiences of the many instructors have been discussed and encapsulated in a document of instructions for new instructors. To avoid disconnection of the various items and their interpretation, the items will be numbered and discussed as presented.

1. We select about ten papers in a subject in which there is a distinct thread of development from one paper to another. The connections between papers must be obvious enough that, with some hints, students will be able to suggest the major experiments in the next paper in the series. If students cannot do this after each paper, you have probably selected a set of papers whose connectedness is clear only to you; in addition, you will have lost a valuable teaching opportunity. The result of having too large a conceptual gap between papers is that students will lose entirely the sense of a story unfolding before their eyes.

It is our experience that the number of papers covered should be at least six, and it is only rarely possible to cover as many as ten. Unless six are studied, the students tend to become bored with later papers, because there is too much emphasis on information. The time spent on individual papers tends to decrease appreciably during the course. The first paper should be used to develop the general biological or biochemical background, and it should therefore be chosen with the digressions fairly well in mind. Digressions which do not genuinely derive from a study of the paper almost invariably produce a negative reaction on the part of the students, even when they are not able to explain that reaction. In cases where they can explain it, they tell you that it is clear that you are lecturing to them on some subject of interest to you, their instructor, and that the students are interested in getting on with the study of the research paper itself. Three to four weeks on the first paper is generally the most that can be spent profitably in terms of student attention. If the first paper is covered very quickly, without being used for developing the general background of the scientist's approach to his work, there is a steadily increasing inability of students to develop the kinds of insights you want from them, even though their words may sound pretty much correct; they will do very poorly when tested on real insight. After the first paper, it is the experience of most instructors that two weeks is about the maximum time that can be spent on one paper before the students become restless. It must be kept in mind at all times that it is not the students' purpose to learn the facts of science but *to go through the acquisition of the insights by the working scientist*. Therefore, since the instructor doesn't have to cover all the meat of any one paper, he can, when student restlessness becomes apparent, just ask permission to explain quickly the remaining unstudied matters that will be of significance to the later papers. (Asking permission of the students to do various things is a stratagem that will be discussed a bit later). (4)

If more than ten papers are covered, it is very likely that the instructor is emphasizing the information in the papers and not the activities of the scientist in getting the information. Thus, the pace of the course of study of biology can be monitored by the instructor by keeping within the range of six to ten papers per semester.

In developing his set of papers, the instructor should first decide the story he wants to have the students learn. Then, he should try to find papers suitable for this story. It not infrequently happens that the connectedness is unattainable at some point for one of several reasons. There may be no paper in the line being studied which gives the needed insight; that is, the insight may have come from another part of biology or from studies with an organism other than the one on which the students will be becoming partial experts. Or, the paper may exist but be too long or too complicated for the students at their stage of learning. It is not necessary to cover a paper in its entirety, so if it is too long, it may be possible to cover just enough of it to get what is needed. Whether the paper is missing or is too long or is too complicated, we now know how to handle this as what is called a technical problem of the method. We prepare a summary of the important results of the missing (or even hypothetical) papers and distribute it to the students. We then go through the first result by asking the students to imagine the experiments that must have been done to permit the first conclusion. With help, the class as a whole will be able to dream up some suitable experiment, even though it may be far from what was actually done. Then, the class proceeds through the list of results, doing each of them experimentally. This has been done also without giving the list of results to the students, but simply presenting the first experimental problem to the class and asking how to do the experiment. When the experiment has been devised, the class is asked to guess the results and explain the guesses. Then, the results of the experiment are given and become, like the explanation of the crime in a detective story, the object of intense interest. (11, 16) The class then suggests the next experiment to be done, and with guidance they indicate the actual next one that was prepared. They then devise the experiment, guess at the results as above, and the procedure is repeated until the major points have been obtained. This latter method is even more profitable than the first, in which the results were distributed. In either case, *in a single class meeting,* instructors can cover the "missing" paper. Experience has shown that this activity is one that should be done in any event, and more than once during the semester, because of its instructiveness to most of the students; it helps them to think actively about how experiments are formulated and executed.

Several attempts have been made to develop two story lines in one class. Thus far, these attempts have not been successful, presumably mainly because the emphasis has shifted from the activity of the scientists to the information obtained by them.

    2. The first paper should be assigned without any discussion of its contents and aim. Students *must* be told at the first class meeting that we know they will understand almost nothing of the first paper and that they are simply to read through it and, if possible, study parts of it for one to two hours before preparing a list of questions covering all words, concepts, techniques, etc., that they do not understand.

This "unprepared" approach to the first paper has already been dealt with in the preceding chapter. The students should be helped to learn to rely on their instructors for answers to questions. Unless they do this, the instructors will not be able to use the class discussion to guide the students along lines that seem to him profitable; the initiative for discussions should, under all conditions, come from the students.

    3. Getting the students to ask questions is a skill that each teacher develops in his own way. Students who remain silent can be helped to begin talking and questioning by arranging a reading assignment which is to be done in pairs or in groups of more than two students as the instructor desires. In such groupings, a silent student should be associated with talking students and in the subsequent class discussions, the silent one can be asked for questions or comments; since the group will have prepared the way, it is usually not difficult to get the silent student to start ask-

ing questions. A few repetitions of the grouping activity should solidify the new-found capacity for talking and questioning.

This grouping device is one that is used by many teachers in kindergarten and grade schools. It is just as valuable at the college level. It should be stressed that no pressure should be applied to the silent student; if he doesn't want to open up with questions, another member of his group should be asked to begin.

4. If you find you're talking more than half the time, you're talking too much. Stop lecturing and give the course back to the students.

It is very easy to fall into the trap of explaining many things. If the instructor keeps in mind that he is not trying to convey information but to help the student learn to analyze the activity of science, he will tend to refrain from talking too much.

5. The temptations to digress to interesting and instructive materials *should* be indulged. But, the instructor must remember that the students are trying to understand the particular paper. You are probably just titillating the students with your stories if you are not back working on the paper, say, every ten minutes.

The role of digressions has been set forth already, as well as the reasons for setting the upper limit at about ten minutes. The added stress of this fifth point is on the fact that the students think the purpose of the course is to get them to understand the papers. After they have developed the higher level of abstractive ability, they will come to recognize that the more interesting and even exciting part of their learning has to do with understanding how scientists think about problems. (1, 3) They can only be helped to achieve this if the instructor is careful to limit his information-conveying digressions so that the real focus of class discussions is the research activity itself.

6. After the first paper it is desirable to prepare the ground for the next paper. Try to get the students to suggest the next experiments to be done before asking them to read the next paper. When you begin the next paper, it is desirable to give

an idea of the over-all problem into which the paper fits, but *under no conditions* should the instructor give a summary of the paper. The students' purpose is not to learn the facts of science but to go through the acquiring of scientific insights.

The reasons for point 6 have been discussed previously, except for the added recommendation that the instructor give an idea of the scientific context of the paper. After the students have, with help from the instructor, proposed some of the next problems to be studied, the instructor can recall the intellectual journey up to that point and thereby help develop the framework of the scientific significance of the entire thread of papers being studied.

7. Don't try to pressure the students to study. No surprise quizzes. No regurgitation-type questions unless the students agree beforehand to such examination questions.

The development of examinations suitable for this course presented a considerable challenge. When students were given questions asking for repetition of previously worked-out analysis, they rebelled against what they called regurgitation-type questions asking, in effect "Why bother to help us learn to think about science if the evaluation of our progress is going to be based on non-thinking-type questions?" (37)

Some instructors have been able to devise situation problems which require student thinking for most or all of the answers. Of course, those are excellent problems and should be encouraged. There are in addition three kinds of examination questions that have developed in association with the course. First, students are given copies of short papers related to the main theme of the course and asked to analyze them in whatever terms the instructor has taught them to analyze papers. Second, we can use the same device used to handle the problem of missing or over-complex papers. That is, we distribute copies of the summary (the real summary or one constructed from the real summary) of a paper related to the main theme of the course and ask the students to reconstruct the experiments and analyses that must have been done to permit the given summary. The third type of examination involves having the individual students study several related papers on his own and present an oral summary of the papers before the class. All three methods work well, but the latter two are preferred by the better students in this course.

There are, however, occasions for some instructors simply to test understanding, whether by a short quiz or a substantial examination. In such situations, we suggest that the students be informed of the instructor's intention well before the actual examination so that they will be able to co-operate to achieve his purpose. The practice of democracy in this course turns out to augment the general level of involvement of the students.

8. No review papers, no text-like materials, and no popular articles (such as from the *Scientific American*) can be used during the first two-thirds of the semester.

During several sections of the course, materials other than scientific papers have been tried. Without exception, when used during the first half of the term, these produce a shutting-off of discussion. Philosophical essays are not quite as damaging. What happens is that, so to speak, students are turned off. They return to their old habits of taking notes, as in lecture courses, rather than participating actively in the thinking and analysis of the work. However, when these text-equivalent materials have been used during the last third of the semester, they seem to do no damage and even seem to stimulate discussions. The interpretation is that such materials can be used safely and with benefit after the students' new working and thinking habits have become firmly established. To play safe, we recommend that essays, too, be deferred until the last third of each semester. This point can be summarized as revealing an extension of Gresham's Law to learning: bad learning habits drive out good ones.

Discussions among instructors at monthly meetings have produced a number of suggestions, which have been collected under the title of hints to consider; these will be placed in the number sequence already begun. No discussion is needed.

9. If you ask students to write any kind of paper or report on any material, write out the assignment yourself beforehand. This, of course, makes sure it is a good assignment. In addition, if you distribute copies of your paper when you return theirs, you will find it helps them enormously to grasp the

kind of thinking you are asking of them. Later assignments can then be given without your having to write a paper yourself.

10. Many times students act bored because, they claim, they know all this. You can quickly check the claim (almost invariably showing it is false) by referring questions by other students to the "bored" one for answers. If he really knows all this, you will have to discover why he is in the course and deal with him individually.

11. The sophistication of upperclassmen is such that they develop skills in the course much faster than first-year students. If there are enough of the former, it may be desirable to place them in a separate section, for early in the course their manifestly quicker understanding tends to inhibit participation by first-year students.

12. Appoint a class secretary to write down questions which the instructor does not want to discuss at the moment they are raised. In this way students feel they will have all their questions answered, since the secretary is instructed to raise these questions when there is some free time later in the course. It is also helpful to make a secretary out of a silent student who thereby frequently begins to participate in discussions. As silent students begin to participate, a new secretary can be chosen from among those still not talking much.

13. It is excellent strategy to inform the students that you will give them their first examination at the end of the first month, that you will grade it and evaluate it and return it *without* recording the grades so that students can learn what kinds of examinations to expect without having the pressure of a recorded grade.

C. RECOMMENDATIONS FOR ENROLLING STUDENTS

Discussions among instructors have also led to the writing of a set of rules distributed to students considering enrollment in this course. There are four items.

1. Students accepted in this course are expected to attend class

meetings, barring illness or other misfortune. If you are the kind of person who is casual about such matters, please don't waste your time and ours by enrolling in this course. Other students could take your place with profit to all concerned.

2. Students enrolled in this course are expected to participate in class discussions. This is not a course for voyeurs. If you are the silent type, please be silent in some other course.

3. The instructors know that the initial phases of this course are difficult for students. You will help yourself maximally by coming to class with lists of questions which you will ask the instructor no matter how silly or dumb the questions may seem to you.

4. Students in this course are expected to inform the instructor as soon as possible if they don't "get the idea." Give your instructor the chance to help you before you get hopelessly behind.

Item 1 derives from the finding that it is virtually impossible to "make-up" missed classes because everything that happens develops during the class meetings. Presumably students who attend reasonably regularly can "make-up" the occasional missed class because they get the idea of the course from attending and participating in the majority of the sessions. We have had ample experience with the casual attender, and the consequences show up at once in the performances on the various kinds of examinations. These students are able to give back factual information at a respectable rate, mainly because the direct information content (that is, not including the digressions) apparently can be memorized or possibly even understood to some extent because there is so little of it: reading six to ten papers in one semester means reading only fifty to seventy pages. However, even a casual reading of the student answers to questions on these pages reveals that they have learned virtually nothing about the activity called science. As our skill in devising new kinds of examinations has developed, these casual students have become incapable of handling examinations. Thus, it is important to weed out such students before they enroll. It might be objected that our results are thus biased by selecting the cow-like students who normally attend all classes. In fact, although this could be the situation, it is not, simply because we do not take attendance, do not require attendance, and put very little pressure on the students to do anything.

Why, then, do we include the item? It is simply to inform students about the instructional needs of the course. Just the fact that it is down in black and white ensures a greater initial degree of co-operation and participation. And, once the initial period is over, we find students attending without compulsion of any kind. Indeed, the nearly 100 per cent attendance is a constant feature of this type of course, and has been found even during student strikes when most classes go virtually unattended. This latter fact is the kind of evidence supporting the statement that students attend these classes with virtually no compulsion at all.

The second item has been the subject of much discussion by our instructors. We do not want to make students feel uncomfortable in the course, and there are some (10–20 per cent) who still say almost nothing in class. We don't bother such students, other than in low-pressure ways described in discussing the information for the instructors. We know, from evaluative sessions, that most of the silent students claim to have benefitted substantially from the course; our examination of them tends to confirm their claim. Those of us who wanted to omit this item pointed out just the fact described—the gain by the silent students—and wanted to avoid excluding them. As always, the issue has been decided experimentally. We seem to have excluded almost no one by this item, for the proportion of silent students isn't noticeably lower than before the distribution of this student information sheet. The reason that the item is retained is that it roughly doubled the fraction of students participating in class discussions in the first weeks. Thus, this one item has accelerated the over-all development of the course by an appreciable amount. Again, we feel that seeing the printed adjuration to participate has evoked a response that mere words of an instructor never seem to evoke. As for the constant proportion of silent students, it can be supposed that the grapevine has let it be known that, in fact, there is no discrimination against and no pressure put on students who choose to remain silent.

Item 3 has effected a variety of reactions from nothing at all to occasionally unleashing some overtalkative (and usually not-so-bright) student. The more mature the students, the more this item seems to yield the desired results, for older students seem less fearful of exposing their ignorance or of saying something stupid. Nevertheless, we feel the printed item helps because students who have troubles are frequently helped to start asking questions by having the item pointed out to them when they come to see instructors during office hours.

The fourth item is self-explanatory. We keep it in the information sheet on the hypothesis that no one is repelled by it and perhaps occasionally some student may be given the extra push needed to get him to go talk with his instructor. We know that most students having trouble with this course have first gone to some of the biology majors for help, and have had essentially no help because these majors do not, themselves, have the ability to read papers. As the curriculum is revised so that science students get a similar early training, the usefulness of biology majors will increase. Our students presently find it necessary to use graduate students in biology to get substantial help. We may decide to establish tutoring sessions with graduate students, but most instructors believe they should do the helping themselves so as to avoid misunderstandings which would derive from different emphases by different tutors.

The question of grades remains to be discussed. At present, this continues to be decided by the individual instructor. Nevertheless, I try to indicate to new instructors that they should have considered the following procedure. At the first class meeting, indicate to students that attendance at the majority of class meetings will almost surely suffice for passing the course. Those who do more than just attend—that is, who participate at all actively—are likely to be given honor grades (A's or B's). The reason for the "weasel-words" *almost surely* and *likely* is that the contemporary university community could not condone giving passing grades for mere attendance because it assumes (for the most part correctly) that physical presence is no indication of learning. Yet, in sections in which this ethic has been promulgated, about two-thirds of the students work hard and do well, and most of the others do enough to make the instructor feel entirely at ease in giving passing grades. There remains a small fraction of students, perhaps two or three in each section, who attend classes, do nothing much, and who would receive passing grades under the scheme as indicated. My own attitude is that the good atmosphere for learning for 80–90 per cent of the students is worth the price of having fewer than a handful "receive something for nothing." Because this course is a terminal one, the cost of this gift will not be visited upon the instructors in later courses. There is no basis for speculation about whether the psychological cost to these fortunate students may be their compulsion to work harder in other courses to ease their consciences for having accepted the gift.

CHAPTER V

Evaluation and Inferences

As each section has finished its semester's work, it has been interviewed to obtain evaluations and comments. Not surprisingly, the students are especially happy with the small class size and its much enhanced intellectual contact between student and instructor. (21) Another factor is the gently introduced necessity for the students to do much or most of the analytical thinking themselves. Yet another positive factor is the feeling that the students have been in contact with "real science" (7) instead of the textbook type of assertion found not only in texts but also in the best of lectures by the best of lecturers.

There has rarely been any criticism, let alone criticism that was shared by a substantial number of students. Indeed, the only frequently repeated "criticism" has been a most surprising and welcome request for a laboratory course to be associated with the class meetings so that students can try for themselves some of the experiments and perhaps some of the original ideas that always come to students during class discussions of even the most esoteric points of some papers.

A rather peculiar "criticism" voiced during meetings with the students is that we have not arranged to use this type of course as the introductory course for every department. This idea will be discussed in a later chapter. Here it suffices to say that the social science equivalent of this course had been devised during its first-year trial in biology.

There have been numerous comments by the students. A highly significant one is the virtually unanimous agreement that the first paper should be given to the students without any preparation by the instructor. The reasons for this opinion are especially suggestive in terms of their implications for learning by such students. As one student put it, the student should be faced immediately with the enormity of the crime he has committed by enrolling in such a course. That is, the reading of real scientific research papers by untrained and uninterested students is such an implausible technique for education that the student should immediately face the full range of the work expected of him.

A second reason is that students have been so spoon-fed in schools up to this point in their lives that there is no way for them to slide gracefully out of the high chair into the hot seat of valid scholarly activity. The process is formally akin to withdrawal symptoms experienced by drug addicts. Many students ask for help in the form of texts or other printed materials, and talk about these hypothetical materials in the way one talks about any familiar crutch. Yet, after a few weeks, most students stop using these materials (which are placed on reserve in the library).

There are far-reaching implications of the demonstrated ability of first-year non-science students to study published research materials. Normally, such students are filled with information in their major subjects for their entire undergraduate careers. It is only in the fourth year or frequently not even until in graduate school that the vast majority of students is exposed to significant extents to the nature of scholarship or research in their major subjects. By this time it is not at all improbable that their heads are so full of loosely structured information that its organization or reorganization is difficult. In our new method, students are first introduced to the nature of the intellectual activities in their subjects and, as suggested by the students in evaluative conferences, this might be a better way of initiating the study of all subjects. That is, we should turn the instructional sequence upside down and give all first-year students what is now thought of as a graduate research seminar in the various fields of study.

At this point it is worthwhile to reconsider the fact that students respond very positively to reading research papers whereas text-like materials cut off discussion. The difference is that the research papers present what is closely related to the actual *activities* of the scientists, whereas text materials present the *information* and *insights* gained by these activities. At least two important inferences may be drawn from consideration of these assertions.

First, the closer the studies come to the experiences and events on which generalizations are based, the greater the student response. (14) It appears to be well known in educational circles that experience-based learning is preferable at all initial stages of learning and at many of the advanced stages. It is not at all clear what the needs of college age students in the United States would be if they had been experience-educated up to that point. The insight to be drawn at this juncture is that a remedial course for college students must return to the experience-based structure if it is to evoke the response to fundamentals that should have been firmly entrenched long before that stage. It follows that one of the major failings of our educational structure as presently organized is that it departs from experience (i.e. it focuses on abstractions) too early for most children. This departure begins, in the United States, in approximately the third grade so that it is to that grade that curriculum developers should turn for the initiation of reforms which should produce the greatest improvement in the quality of the education in the United States.

Second, it is not the information that is so entrancing to students but the activity producing that information. (39) This point has been found repeatedly in the classroom as the students have been encouraged to think about the informational contents of papers only to find them uninterested. Indeed, as mentioned previously, many students who are much excited about our course, nevertheless don't care for the actual subject of the course. This indifference to subject plus fascination with activities add up to the important inference that grade-school curriculum reforms which focus on presenting information in a novel, clear, and exciting way are doomed to fail of their over-all objective simply because students are early interested only in activities and not in information. At some age (probably at the time of puberty) students become capable of and interested in abstractions and information. "Turned-off" students have to be treated as though they were lower-graders in this respect. Indeed, we seem to see here that to reorientate the older student we have to return him to the education problem that he failed to resolve as a youth. Only then can he retrace the steps and stages needed to structure his development and thinking in a way that will permit him to accept meaningfully the great insights of man's cultural activities developed over the millennia. The Freudianism of this view is quite obvious.

Another way of stating the point of the preceding paragraph is that the human mind develops properly only if each subject is given an experiential basis to permit the mind to fashion its own structure of that subject. Our students have been caused to depart from this orientation at about the third grade. This is the point at which the informational content of school subjects reaches a development of sufficient scope for the adult mind to discover generalizations which simplify the teaching process. As a concrete example, consider the fact that young pupils are faced with knowing how to count money, how to encompass the idea of a shopping list that includes apples plus pears, how to know that he has two grandmothers, etc. The adult mind sees the general insight required as the knowledge of addition, so that the problem of teaching is simplified if the child is taught arithmetic separately and at once so he can handle, as applications of a generalization, his money and fruit and grandparents. This approach is wrong because it should be known that the child should learn addition as the result of one of his actual problems, and that the other problems should also be faced with the same orientation to experience. If the matter is handled in this fashion, the child's own mind will find the generalization that addition works for all objects. Aside from the joy of the discovery, it is essential for the child's mind to practice the development of abstractions for itself because the abstractive capacity is the most important, the most essentially human, and the one least developed by present-day school curricula.

The particular example used (that of arithmetic addition) is only an illustration of what is meant in asserting that adults can find generalizations to force on unprepared young minds. Two consequences of this premature abstraction are (1) that the child's abstractive abilities are depressed and (2) his learning motivation is shut off because he is being given information of a type for which he has no slots. He rejects these inputs in a way entirely similar to that by which he shuts out the physical inputs to a weak eye which is not co-ordinated with the vision of a good eye, if he is forced to make the co-ordination decision too early. These abstractions may be fine for adults, but they do not take into account realistically the needs of the young developing mind. It is as though the mind must itself make the jump from the specific to the general, so that teaching the general postpones, perhaps forever, the young person's developing of that aspect of intuition which, when developed, will permit him to use abstract thinking to leap ahead of experience-based learning.

If the method is restructuring the students' thought processes, why does it fail with 10 to 20 per cent of the students? There are at present only two indications of what may be responsible. Our method of using science research papers recapitulates the scientists' activities, but only in a limited sense. For example, there is no real sense of the fumbling around that occurs in practice. Scientists don't record such things. Perhaps a more important point is that the actual failures are not displayed, so the students don't get the insights which derive from doing something wrong and puzzling over the significance of the failure. If such aspects could be included, it is very likely that the success percentage would increase. It is less certain that it would increase very much because it is a rather firm impression that almost all of the students who don't like our course are among the less intelligent students. Some, to be sure, have been very bright, but they seem to have been the exceptions in this respect.

The omission of failures is something that would be remedied if we could devise a suitable laboratory course to be associated with the research papers course. Indeed, as mentioned at the very beginning of this report, it would be preferable to give students a real research and development laboratory course from the beginning. Actual experimentation normally differs from cook-book laboratory courses in that the failures are much more instructive.

Yet another reason for failing with some students is that they are taking three or four other courses at the same time. In a sense, these other courses may be undoing our remedial work by permitting the old habits to remain unchallenged. These courses thus play the same role as the too-early introduction of text-like materials. This point could be studied experimentally if our approach could be expanded to include all the courses normally taken by first-year students.

The relationship between students and teachers also contains significant potential implications. Courses are normally taught by single instructors, and, for a subject as broad as biology, it is manifestly unlikely that any one person is equally expert in all phases of the subject matter. For example, if the instructor is a plant physiologist, it is not likely that he can deal at all expertly with Drosophila genetics. Similarly, a molecular biologist will be far beyond his depth when he deals with animal organ systems. As a result, students taught by such instructors are being exposed to a highly uneven or heterogeneous level of insights. It is likely that student reaction to this situation produces, perhaps subconsciously, significant differences in ability to grasp the material in question; students simply sense the relative ignorance of the instructor who is talking about matters concerning which he has only textbook knowledge. (30)

In the new method, each instructor teaches what he knows best. The method is self-limiting because even the digressions by the individual instructor will be those apparent to the instructor and therefore those for which his knowledge can be presumed to be more than at the textbook level. Thus, although the students receive a less-balanced or less broad coverage of biology, the information that is actually presented has the ring of authoritative knowledge and is also contained within a structure of relationships that makes evident sense to the instructor and therefore to the students. (15)

That the argument of the preceding two paragraphs is correct receives support from the responses of students to what the instructors do in class. We try to get each instructor to include at least one paper of which he is an author. Every one who does this remarks on the abrupt increase in the level and quality of the class discussions. Talking with students during evaluation sessions always elicits remarks about the greater interest or excitement and greater insights when the subject was the instructor's own research work.

A point that has not been described in any detail is the nature of the sequel courses that students have requested after each semester. Two instructors have had ideas they wanted to try, and these trials will be described briefly. First, it must be stressed that students in such courses tend to be the brighter students, at least because they have done well in the first course; they are generally also among the very brightest students in their own major departments.

Both colleagues tried the use of more advanced materials. One chose a recent series of papers which led to a rather complete understanding of a whole area of biology. The other trial focused on the experiments in an area in which the activity is still extremely high because the basic problems have not yet been clarified and solved. These two instructors and a number of their students concluded that the trials both succeeded in producing good courses that were appreciated by the students but that neither course had developed a format or approach which made its continuation desirable.

The students in these sequel courses have a higher-than-average ability to read and understand research papers; one colleague experimented with this aspect to the point of discovering that students could handle a paper per day (that is, three per week) with the same degree of efficiency that the previous semester's classes had handled one per week. Further, the complexity of the papers that can be studied without student complaint is obviously greater; this finding is further support for the belief that the students are really developing expertise in problem analysis.

A very important inference may be drawn from the experiences with the sequel courses: one semester is enough to effect most of the enhanced competence that our approach can evoke. (12) Continuation along the same lines doesn't seem worthwhile. Thus, once the students have mastered the analytical approach and have had their curiosity about biology reawakened, they now are ready to deal with a greater amount of information put in an abstract way. (17) Another way of stating this inference is that in students of this age the capacity for abstraction is very close to the surface of the mind and needs very little development of an experiential base before the higher abstractive qualities of the mind begin to work and to need feeding. This inference is extremely important because it could mean that the damage done by conventional teaching can be relatively quickly repaired by exposure of the students to well-chosen remedial courses. It could further mean that the repair need be done for no more than the first year of college, leaving the existing framework of college curricula without drastic changes, other than those discovered by curriculum development projects.

Of course, these last inferences derive from the results with the highly selected group of better students at our university, and our students are already so selected that the average student is in the top 10 per cent of high school seniors in the United States. People who may choose to experiment with students outside these highly selective limits would do well to keep in mind the possibility that the approach may not work with less capable students or, even if it works, it may take much longer and require a much more complex set of conditions.

This chapter will be concluded with a discussion of the extent to which our results bear on the problems set forth in the book by Bruner on the results of the 1959 Woods Hole Conference on Education. Four themes were set forth, one of which has already been discussed. Our students' understanding of the scientists' activities is a fact giving direct support to the second theme which may be summarized as asserting that the foundations of any subject may be taught to anybody at any age; the basic ideas and themes are as simple as they are powerful. Thus, experience may be showing that schools are wasting precious years by postponing teaching of many important subjects because they appear too difficult. Our experiences support the conclusion insofar as it would assert that 17-year-old students can grasp competently the foundations of complex aspects of both classical and modern biology and biochemistry. (5)

The third theme elaborated by Bruner concerns the question of intuition, and asks if school children can be led to master the technique of arriving at the plausible but tentative formulations without going through the analytical steps by which such formulations would be found to be valid or invalid conclusions. There is no question about the ability of our college-age students to do this, and in a field far removed from their own interests. The relevance of our experimentation rests on the inference that the point is achieved in our method by focusing students' attention on the details of scientific research activities and permitting the students to develop the intuitive insights and skills without discussing the problem at all.

The fourth theme is no more than the raising of the question of how to stimulate the desire to learn. (29) The Conference could do nothing substantial with this question. I should like to digress at this point to discuss one aspect of the question of why there are few, if any, suggested solutions to many of the important problems being discussed by educators. It is readily discovered by simply skimming through pages of books by Piaget, Bruner, and others that much of the experimentation is done with mathematical subjects as test objects. I believe it is likely that the study of the learning of mathematics will turn out to be largely unrewarding in terms of insights given into learning of most subjects. The reasoning can be set forth in one sentence: By and large we do not experience most mathematics. This means that most experiences are of such a nature that their mathematical aspects are chiefly abstractions. What do we experience when we add two blocks of wood to two other blocks of wood? Do we experience the quality of increased weight or increased number in such a way that we feel things to be twice as heavy or as numerous? When we buy material for a suit or a dress do we experience areas as products? It is probable that mathematics is not direct or first-order experience; rather it is second-order experience and therefore belongs more to the world of abstraction than do the phenomena of nature and of direct observation.

Apart from this digression, there is an inference related to the fourth theme. It derives from experiments with varying degrees of pressure in the classroom. The consequences were that application of pressure to learn or to study brought results inversely related to the pressure (22). Thus, one may conjecture that the way to get students to learn is to let them learn. This point was taken up earlier, and quantitatively, because the pressure level in our method is a technical parameter about which we now have some information. However, there are other remarks related to the question of pressure. One concerns the oft-quoted maxim that we shouldn't sacrifice the child to the adult. Pressure levels are determined by what the adult wants to achieve. The achievement of some successes tends to obscure the fact that students should not necessarily be expected to perform well as a result of stimuli that are both obvious and of significance to adults. The end result of classroom pressure on children is adult disengagement. Since we cannot foresee the world in which the student will work and live as an adult, a pre-eminent educational problem is to avoid fitting him only for the current world. Further, the student should be brought to the frontiers of insight and knowledge as quickly as possible so he can begin his transcendence of the capacities of the current world. (20) Therefore, we should avoid requirements deriving from the (usually) unformulated and unconscious belief that students should recapitulate the intellectual development of their elders. In a real sense, those who follow the same paths tend to fall into the same bogs. If we really believe that young people will transcend us, there is no escape from facing them early with problems that we faced as adults; not the information we have gained but the problems we have met and, to some extent, solved. This transcendence cannot be achieved through compulsion. Either the new activity is so worth doing that young people reach out for it of their own accord, or the new vistas set before them are not worth the effort of the young. (13) In the latter case, no amount of pressure will help. We have always deceived ourselves into thinking pressure works, because a respectably large fraction of young students performs well. In fact, these students are already internally motivated and there is virtually nothing adults can do to divert them from using their minds and capacities in a reasonably effective way. The level of achievement of current teaching should be taken as the base line or reference line above which lie the teaching and curriculum effectiveness for which we are striving. Problems can be presented to the young, but unless they are seen as problems by the young, no amount of pressure will cause them to be seen as other than obstacles. It is only after serious abstractive capacity has been developed that the nature of the pressure can be understood and not reacted to negatively.

CHAPTER VI

New Applications of the Method

Up to this point the discussion has been entirely of the development of a biological science course for non-scientists. The preceding chapters have set forth the reasons for believing that the research studies method generates intellectual excitement by allowing student association with professional intellectual activities. There are also substantial indications of release of students from intellectual repression that had covered up the natural stores of curiosity about nature and motivation to study. These inferences are so far-reaching, if valid, that it became necessary to explore the applicability (with suitable adaptations) to other problems of education. This chapter sets forth the spectrum of new applications being studied and, since all are in partially incomplete form, gives what is best described as a set of progress reports.

1. BIOLOGY MAJORS

A priori, there seemed few reasons why the basic course should not be as useful for potential biologists as for the non-biologists. The major such reason probably is that students already oriented toward science will have developed (by themselves or because of their greater interest in high school science courses) the problem-oriented attitude that is so characteristic a result of our first course. Since the attitude of our work is empirical, it was decided to try the experiment by asking for volunteers from among the several dozen prospective biology majors among the entering first-year students. The upshot was that eleven students came to the course as volunteers, taking an extra course, and with no credit. These conditions were not entirely satisfactory, but arose out of various aspects of the red tape in which our department was enmeshed at the time.

To permit as direct a comparison of results as possible, it was decided to use exactly the same set of research papers used with non-science students in the preceding semester. To be sure, the commitment of science majors, coming without rewards to an extra course, had to be greater even than that of the entire group of science majors coming to one of their regular courses for which credits were given; therefore, the results could be expected to be more favorable because of the greater commitment. On the other hand, the "extra" and non-credit aspects of the experiment could be expected to result in a decreased activity. In the actual event, both expectations were fulfilled, and about half of the students appeared regularly without having done much work but apparently with appreciable interest and with profit to themselves merely as observers. The other students were manifestly very captivated by the class and told me that they ended up doing more work for this voluntary course than for their other courses. The differences in class performances of these two groups of students were very marked.

There were two markedly different aspects of this course for serious students of science. First, it was much easier to teach because one could talk in a much more complex way without having to choose words as carefully as with the non-science students. Mathematics could be used without being concerned about possible panic in the classroom. And, these science majors had backgrounds not officially much different from those of the non-science majors. The ease was due entirely to their own greater feeling for matters scientific and mathematical.

The second difference was in the pace of the class. It was initially puzzling and discouraging to note the fact that, judging by the rate at which papers were covered, this class was going only about two-thirds as fast as the non-science students. This might have been attributed to the fact that it was an extra course for which the students were doing little homework. But, it soon developed that half the class was deeply involved with the course, as set forth above. Even these students were going slower. The explanation emerged when reconsideration of the contents of class discussions showed that these students were so much more interested in the science itself and its ramifications that the number and extent of the digressions were considerably greater. These students simply insisted on learning more factual biology along with whatever they were getting out of studying the papers. Since the emphasis on information violates the orientation of the course, it became necessary to speed up the coverage of papers after realizing this. It is hard to do because of student resistance, but it can be done. This is obviously a point to challenge us in the future versions of the course for science majors.

After about seven weeks of the thirteen-week semester had passed there chanced to be a speaker at our weekly departmental colloquium who was to talk about his research, which was closely related to the research in the papers the class was studying. The entire class was asked if it wished to attend but the invitation was made especially clear to the five students whose class performances had set them very much apart from the other six. The result of their attendance was not easy to assess, because they lacked some straight factual information. Nevertheless the students maintained that they understood more than half of the colloquium talk, and each student separately asserted that it was surprisingly easy for him to figure out the next experiment before the lecturer actually described it. The fact that they volunteered this claim independently seems highly significant, for it is precisely at this point that should be found any ability of our methods to effect a student's ability to transcend us. To say this directly, if this method really alters student reasoning ability, the alteration should show up in what is most practiced—working out the next step in a paper. Then, if students in their first year in college can develop this capacity in seven weeks, it seems that they have an ability which clearly surpasses their instructor's ability to do that same thing.

From that week on, several of the students felt inclined to attend the weekly colloquium even though the subjects of the various lecturers (all from other colleges) were not all related to the main subject of our research papers. The students were not further examined on what they got out of the lectures, but it is evident that they must have understood quite a bit to make it both worthwhile and interesting for them to attend. There is no control group. Yet, it seems remarkable that 17-year old prospective biology majors, after only seven weeks of college can, with profit, attend graduate colloquia. These students are in their seventh week of first-year chemistry and mathematics, they have studied on the college level *no* physics, organic chemistry, biochemistry, or biology.

The apparently successful course led the students to ask what they should do next. After discussions with my colleagues these students were allowed to enroll in two intermediate courses—genetics and marine biology—which would be taught by professors familiar with the kinds of activities of our first course. Our students could be expected to have big gaps in their biological information, so it was decided to make tutors available several days per week to give the students quick information they would otherwise have had to dig out from textbooks in the library.

The results of these courses have been evaluated by discussions with several of the students involved and with the instructors. The instructors asserted that several of these students were very much better prepared than the other students (mainly third-year students) who took the course in the normal sequence. Particularly impressive was their ability to get to the heart of problems very quickly.

Several of the students made it known during the semester that the courses seemed to be a bit slow. Apparently, their ability to take in information was appreciably greater than that of the other students, despite the very much broader and longer preparation of those other students. In a later discussion with the students, they maintained that they could detect one ability in which they were superior: they could determine with confidence when they understood something and when they didn't understand. This ability permitted them to use their instructor quickly and efficiently to clear up their questions. As a result, they had few questions that were not handled within the classroom. Therefore, the tutorial sessions became virtually an agency for the students to explore new aspects of the subjects which were not being covered in the course itself. The idea of such a broadening kind of tutorial situation is an interesting one in itself, and we will consider it on its own merits. However, from the point of view of support for the supposedly "uninformed" graduates of our new first-year course, it is evident that the tutorials are not needed and will, therefore, be discontinued.

There is another question about biology majors. Can the insights from the first course be used to improve the existing intermediate and advanced courses? All the work on this question has been done by my colleagues, especially those involved with me in working on preparing instructors from southern colleges to try our new methods. These colleagues became sufficiently impressed with the possibilities of using research papers extensively to alter their own intermediate courses substantially. The new courses can be roughly described as using appropriate research papers to demonstrate the origin and definition of significant new concepts or insights into biology. Then, the instructor lectures more or less as he previously did until some other important new aspect is needed. He uses the relevant papers to give the students the understanding of the aspect and how it arose, and again returns to lecturing. In this fashion, students are made acquainted with the experimental origins and understanding of the major aspects of these courses and then are able to use their well-grounded understanding to handle more expertly the didactic nature of the rest of the course.

One colleague, Dr. Edgar Zwilling, used these tactics in his course for fourth-year students of embryology. He, too, felt strongly that his students were very much better grounded than with his previous all-lecture method. But, he was aware of the fact that the use of the papers slowed up the class appreciably so that he would be unable to cover as many parts of the subject as previously. Although he felt that the gain by his hybrid method far outweighed the loss of a few topics, he decided to try to solve the problem of the missing topics. He developed what he called the symposium method, which has the students preparing talks on a few papers, each covering one of the missing topics. In this way, he hoped to get the students to understand the topics far better than if he tried to lecture on the topic briefly in the class meetings. The result was that the students were so pleased to be able to develop the missing topics themselves that most, if not all, of them read a dozen or more papers each and insisted on holding extra meetings at night so that each student would have enough time to present his topic decently. Professor Zwilling ended up staging three symposia in three weeks, and his class thereby covered—out of its own desire to work—appreciably more subject matter than ever before in his teaching of this course. The extremely basic nature of the appeal of the actual scientific activity as revealed by the published papers is made manifest by the response of these advanced students.

As a result of the response of Professor Zwilling's students to the first of the symposia, the idea of adapting it for the first-year students was discussed, and several instructors tried it at the end of the semester. There seems little doubt that the symposium will be incorporated widely at our university because of the very high level of interest and learning on the part of students preparing these symposium talks. Its use as an examination device has been discussed in a preceding chapter.

The general structure of departmental offerings is now likely to include an introductory course in how science is done (our first-year course) followed by these hybrid intermediate and advanced courses using papers plus lectures. Lecture courses will continue to be taught by those who prefer to lecture or who remain unconvinced that studying research papers is more than a superficial way of titillating students. Since not all of us are good lecturers and since not all of us can handle students studying research papers, this seems to be the most efficient way to employ the combined talents of a heterogeneously gifted faculty.

There have been two trials of the methods with science students in other countries. Both trials, for scheduling reasons, have been with students in the second and third years at the university; the courses were given at Oxford University in England and at Tel Aviv University in Israel. The results were similar at the two institutions. These advanced students knew so much biology that the information in the papers tended to be known to them. Therefore, there was a certain impatience with playing the game of pretending not to know the outcome of the entire set of papers. This problem was handled by shifting to a set of very recent papers. It could equally well be handled by using a biological subject entirely unfamiliar to the students in question. Because of the familiarity with the particular field of biology, the course became more nearly one in analysis of experiments than in analysis of the activities of the experimenter.

Students at Tel Aviv University filled out a questionnaire and were also participants in a discussion of the course. By the subjective criteria of the permanent faculty of the department and from the students' responses, it was determined that the course was highly successful in producing an analytical and experiment-oriented group of students. A special test in design of experiments showed an enormously greater capacity of these students, who were compared with the fourth-year students in the same department who had taken no such course. The department concluded that the course should become a permanent feature of its curriculum and should be placed in the first-year program when scheduling permits. There is already some restructuring of advanced courses based on the altered orientation and capacities of the students.

2. TEACHING IN COLLEGES IN WHICH RESEARCH IS NOT STRESSED

As has been pointed out in the section on background of the course, the new approach was designed for reversing the flight from teaching in institutions in which the level of research activity was so high that the research scientists were doing very little teaching. It is probably reasonably accurate to guess that this is the situation in about 10 per cent of the more than 2000 college-level institutions in the United States. In the others, there are varying combinations of heavy teaching loads and non-research-oriented faculties. In many institutions a major fraction of faculty people has no research degrees. How can this method be used in, for example, colleges in which faculties with master's degrees are teaching many hours per week and in which the class size is many times the 25 students per class that we consider maximal?

A pragmatic attitude on this question is to consider the points one by one as problems to be worked on experimentally and, hopefully, solved. Thus, the first problem is what can be done about the fact that most college teachers are simply not qualified to teach research papers, not because of any necessarily lesser intelligence or commitment, but rather because of restrictions in their youthful possibilities of going through to research degrees.

It is no secret that all curriculum development projects have found their major obstacle to be the work of retraining the teachers. It is equally well known that teachers, being human, exhibit great inertia when it comes to altering styles and methods which have suited them in the past. How much more difficult should the retraining problem be for someone wanting to do this with college-level teachers when the source of the problem includes the additional hurdle of having to raise the research background of the teacher? To retrain high school teachers requires far less by way of adding to their knowledge than does trying to give a research orientation to college teachers who have never experienced the tortures and delights of science research.

At the time I was considering this problem, I was asked by chance to serve as a consultant on a curriculum development project sponsored by the Institute for Services to Education (ISE). Their Curriculum Resources Group (CRG) was working on the problem that arose from the use of typical courses and texts in Southern Negro colleges for the slow-reading student with a relatively poor school background. The result, according to CRG personnel, was that the youngsters fell still further behind the northern student with good reading skills and a relatively superior high-school preparation. They wanted to know if the curriculum could be improved to the point of helping their students overcome their handicap, at least to the point of not falling further behind. In addition, the CRG wanted to tackle the problem in colleges not generally considered to be of first-line quality among Negro colleges. This challenge is captivating all by itself, but after some hours of meetings with the CRG personnel (which included some of the biology instructors from these colleges) it became very clear how great are the differences between courses emphasizing new teaching and learning methods rather than curriculum development. The CRG had been in existence for an entire year at the time of contact with me, and the results with biology were considered positive, but not so much that the group didn't want to look at other interesting and possibly relevant experimentation in college biology teaching. Consequently, when it was proposed that our new course method be tried for the 13 colleges involved, the CRG was interested enough to ask how to handle the problems outlined at the start of this section.

The problem of training of the teachers appeared to have a "built-in" solution. We would use the summer to give them an intense research seminar on the general topic on which they would base their set of papers. To be specific, most of the teachers actually involved considered their strongest preparation and interest to be in animal physiology. We would select, with help from the teachers, a set of ten papers that would tell a reasonable story. Then, we would get a physiologist to run a 5 days per week 3 hours per day research-paper seminar covering perhaps forty papers, among which would be the ten papers to be used for the students. In this way, the teachers would have an intense research studies experience in the precise area in which they would subsequently work with the students. If the teachers could manage a respectable performance with just this theoretical preparation, then during the following summer we should place each of them in a research laboratory actively working on just those kinds of problems. In that way we would first make them into "paper experts" and then into real experts in one field of research.

It was also evident that this way of developing a new curriculum for the thirteen colleges would have the added merit of intense training of the teachers which could not but help their teaching capacities, even if the attempt to use the research studies method turned out to be a failure.

There was not, at the initial stage, any reason to be concerned about the number of students per class. Teachers working in this program were relieved of appreciable amounts of teaching in order to focus their attention on developing the new curriculum which the ISE expected to spread to other colleges with the same problems. Eventually, colleges would have to face the problem of teaching loads and class sizes. The attitude was to wait until some curriculum had been developed that achieved the goals of the ISE, and then let the administration worry about how to utilize it. There was no point in anticipating an administration's financial problem unless, and until, there was something new that was so good that for reasons of quality instruction its adoption problems had to be met head on. After all, if two summers were to be spent on this method it was entirely possible that the adaptations that would surely develop could well permit someone to figure out how to solve these other problems.

Because the teachers indicated two different main interests (animal physiology and molecular genetics) we held a research seminar in the former during July and a seminar in the latter topic during August. Teachers concentrated on their preferred seminar while gaining a less intensive familiarity with the other. In retrospect, this was not a good decision because the intensity of the needed commitment is so great that it would have been better to have given the separate groups each a two-month research seminar. For much of July these teacher-students were just getting orientated toward the kind of thinking needed for the topics. However, it still seems that summer research seminars of this intensity constitute an excellent method for upgrading college teachers with this background, and it would be wise to establish centers to which teachers could go every summer for this kind of experience. For many teachers, the experience will serve as an inducement to return to graduate studies to obtain the research experience and degrees that will enrich their lives and the lives of their students.

During the summer, the CRG brought to the seminars ten boys and girls who would be entering some of the thirteen colleges as freshmen in the fall. These students worked with all teacher groups (there were others working on physics, English, social sciences, and mathematics) mostly permitting the teachers to try out their new curriculum ideas. For $2\frac{1}{2}$ weeks the research papers method was demonstrated by working with these students while the teachers observed. Then, for $1\frac{1}{2}$ weeks, the teachers tried their hands at running one class period, each using these same students. The major result of the teachers' working with the students seemed to be that they lost their fear of starting the discussion of research papers with the students.

It had been made explicitly clear by the teachers before the summer program was agreed upon, that no more than one of them had much hope for the method. The reason for trying it was that they had come to recognize that working on curriculum changes alone could not be expected to bring about more than minor improvements, and that it might be just as well to attempt a very large improvement in the quality of the biology teaching. By the end of the summer seminars it seemed that several teachers still felt much the same pessimism about the prospects of succeeding with this method, but were willing to attempt it if modified. The others were appreciably less pessimistic, and they too intended to try various adaptations on their students.

The results of the first term's efforts can be inferred from the proceedings of a conference of all personnel of the various CRG programs held in Atlanta in November 1968 and from impressions gained during observation visits to two of the thirteen colleges during the week preceding the Atlanta Conference. At the conference, it was my impression that the teachers generally felt that there were good points to the method in their hands, but that by and large they had not achieved the same degree of success that I had. The teacher from a school whose students averaged less than eighth grade in reading level had been forced to abandon the papers because the students couldn't read them. She had decided to try using reprints from *Scientific American*. Other teachers reported variable degrees of student interest and performance, and several teachers reported that many of their students had indicated that they preferred the papers to texts because all one could get out of texts was facts, and they weren't the real objects of such a course.

My personal observations gave me somewhat greater confidence in the eventual usefulness of the method in these colleges. At the first college I went to, a class of 21 students discussed a paper for 1½ hours with 14 students taking a very active and informed part in the discussions; the others contributed virtually nothing. The main flaw in the teacher's performance was total lack of use of digressions, so that the course was developing only the information and thread of argument available in the papers. The teacher was unaware of this flaw until it was pointed out; it can be supposed that a resultant broader course content would bring some of the more silent students into the discussion. Given its narrowness, the class discussion I observed was as good as with my own students—a fact which gives me confidence in the eventual usefulness of the method. At the second college, a similar situation obtained, with the discussions being a bit less inclusive of students, and the instructor doing a very little bit of digression to broaden the discussion. The results of just one year's experience with teachers and students in this program are far better than expected a priori. It seemed unlikely that teachers not at all engaged in biological research could be brought to a level of competence (in 8 weeks) high enough to permit them to achieve something by this method. Yet, I observed at least one impressive and successful class, in which the backgrounds of both teacher and students were certainly no better than average for the thirteen-college group. The intensity and quality of the student discussion revealed first-class minds in many of the students, and showed that the method can elicit first-class thinking in a situation not at all expected to be of this top quality by the CRG people themselves. My personal conclusion is that this method can readily be developed for use at such colleges, so that the applicability is not limited by the intellectual levels of the teachers and students but rather by the administrative constraints discussed earlier. A few years of such courses in these colleges will be needed to permit administrations to evaluate whether the gains by this method are so great that there must be no return to traditional teaching methods. At colleges whose teacher and student attainments are somewhat higher than at these thirteen colleges, it seems unlikely that this method would fail to make the teaching more effective.

3. APPLICATION TO OTHER SUBJECTS

The description of the biological science course can be readily applied to subjects other than biology by substituting the appropriate name for the word biology. What does a biologist do when he's doing biology? Suppose history is substituted for biology. Does the idea make sense? Does the method still work? And, if it works in any sense, is it worthwhile? Is it already being done? —There are obviously many questions that can be asked.

With the aid of the insights and inferences from the experience with the biology course, it was to easy to construct the equivalent course for the social sciences. Happily, among my colleagues and neighbors there are social scientists interested in experimenting with new methods, so it has been possible to get the method tried in economics (and in philosophy by a colleague who had independently evolved a rather similar method of teaching.)

The essential similarity of approach rests on the focus on the *activities* of the social scientists and uses some working paper for digressions to principles and practices of the social science, thereby providing the desired general survey of the subject.

The actual working out of the approach can be gotten from the following excerpt from Professor Richard Weckstein's report to the Brandeis University economics department on the result of

70 A STRATEGY FOR EDUCATION

his trying the method for about seven weeks. His report is entitled "A report on an experiment in teaching introductory economics."

> After 15 years of teaching introductory economics to college
> undergraduates in the more or less traditional ways that have
> come along, I have reluctantly come to the conclusion that
> the text-assisted presentation that is accepted as the standard
> is more gratifying to the compulsive needs of the instructor
> who is a professional economist than it is to the uninitiated
> student who is trying to fathom what economics is and does
> . . . But after being led, by intellectual persuasion, to try a
> radically different approach to introductory economics, I have
> discovered that the neat division of topics and the logic of the
> sequence of their presentation are neither necessary nor do
> they conform to the needs of students who are being intro-
> duced to the subject for the first time. Each student . . . was
> expected to read, "Evaluating Mexican Land Reform" which
> reports the outcome of research I had recently completed. It
> is not written for beginning students and presumes a knowl-
> edge of basic economics. The approach . . . starts the begin-
> ning student off with the material that is a product of the
> working professional instead of some ersatz version, distilled
> off the true product, neatly ordered, and simple. The first few
> class hours were spent in lecturing and informal discussion on
> the general historical background of Mexican agriculture.
> Once the students had had an opportunity to read the paper,
> they used class meetings to explore the arguments of the
> paper so they could understand them and evaluate the
> method and the conclusions. [In practice, the students
> worked over the paper one section at a time] . . . The earli-
> est questions and discussions in class were attempts to under-
> stand the paper in a fairly simple analogue to an engineering
> idea of efficiency . . . The flow of questions, answers and dis-
> cussions then grappled with the ideas required to relate mar-
> ket price to equilibrium price, or value, and particular values
> to their foundations. Much of the time discussions were halt-
> ing and frustrated, but at other times they sparkled and
> occasionally there were breakthrough insights. In the course
> of the 7 weeks . . . most of the ideas that are taken up in an

orderly sequence of a conventional introductory economics course were developed in class and discussed a propos of the problem of evaluating Mexican land institutions. For example, the value of particular goods to individual consumers invoked a discussion of utility theory. The discussions of physical efficiency . . . eventually [led] to the development of the theory of the firm and the determinants of input and output . . . The theory of market price determination and the analysis of competitive industry came along in due course as a necessary link in the understanding of the arguments. And owing to the importance of monopoly in the supply of some inputs and the markets for some of the crops, it was unavoidable that the theory of monopoly and monopsony were developed to the point that the idea of price distortions could be understood . . . By pushing, more could have been squeezed onto the Mexican land reform hook. For example, international values could have been explored a propos of Mexican agricultural inputs and outputs that enter into foreign trade. . . . There was simply never any lack of interest and the early skepticism felt by some dissipated after the first week. Not one student felt either left out or left behind, and participation was remarkably universal. There was always an excess demand for class time. I certainly never took time to lecture because the students were lacking in ideas or questions.

On the basis of performance on a standardized objective examination at the end of the semester the class, which to me seemed an ordinary Brandeis group of students . . . did about as well as they might have been expected to after a conventional course . . . I doubt that they are quite as well versed in the description of the tools of microeconomics as students in standard courses. But I would think they understand more about the uses of the standard tools in applied work.

The results of teaching three sections of an economics course at Northeastern University were similar to those obtained at Brandeis University.

An entirely similar procedure is applicable to others of the social sciences, though the actual class procedures will depend on whether the subject is closer to or further from the natural sciences in its possession of data.

4. ADULT EDUCATION

There are two important differences between teaching adults and college students which make it much more difficult to handle adults. First, any college class is composed of individuals whose intellectual levels, ages, backgrounds, and experiences are extremely homogeneous compared with what is likely to obtain in any group of adults. Second, older people are less able to make radical changes in thought patterns so that it should be much harder for them to adopt an empirical or experiment-oriented approach.

There are two compensating factors in that (1) older people who would become involved in adult education classes are likely to be above average in motivation and (2) motivated adults already have an abstractive capacity (which is unlikely to develop much further.) Therefore, their ability to accept lecturing approaches is very much greater than that of young students. Thus, our method may not be needed at all insofar as its present formulation is largely determined by the need to go from the specific to the general to effect the development of abstract reasoning.

There are, nevertheless, two important reasons for trying out the research studies methods on adults. First, there may be factors operating which will play a more important role than those we have foreseen. Second, it is possible to test some of the inferences from the results with college students, since adults can be expected to behave differently in predictable ways.

A group of 25 adult volunteers was assembled to meet twice weekly evenings for 1½ hours. The number dropped to 19 after the first research paper was distributed, and one other student dropped out; 18 students participated in almost all subsequent classes. The group included several 20-year-old girl secretaries, a few housewives, two workmen, and several professional people, including an industrial engineer with his own firm in a large city.

Three different experiments were tried on this class. First there had always been the prejudice against "discovery papers" which, as implied by the name, are papers presenting a scientific discovery or achievement and very little else. The prejudice was that such papers don't lead anywhere, so that students don't get the sense of the continuing story that makes up the vast majority of scientific developments. Three such papers were used as the first three of the term. It became clear that, although the students learned from the papers and even enjoyed studying them, they acquired no feel for the practice of science. This was indicated by the number of remarks revealing that the students couldn't anticipate what would be done next.

The second experiment was to try very long digressions. If, in fact, adults differ in their acceptance of lecturing approaches, it should be possible to digress in a way that would "turn off" college students. One digression was started with about a half-hour to go in one class, and continued for about one hour of the next class. Almost all the class members accepted the digression with equanimity and interest. It was, therefore, very rewarding to have the youngest member of the class come outside of class hours to protest the last two class meetings. She remarked that she felt increasingly and desperately lost to the point that she felt like running out of the class; she claimed to have lost all sense of what was happening. One of the other young secretaries indicated a similar, though less violent, reaction to these class sessions. The older people in the class with whom the matter was discussed were unable to comprehend the feelings; they had experienced no difficulty with the lengthy digression.

Third, during one evening session, substantial pressure was applied in the form of verbal grading of questions or answers; the result was almost palpable tension for the next few class meetings, even though the discussion level didn't drop off as is usually the case with the first-year students. A few of the students were absent during this period.

The over-all results of the experiment were obtained from an evaluative session with the students. The success of the experiment was attested to by all the students, and most went on to add that the involvement with "real science research papers" was a key feature. In addition, there was great appreciation of the opportunity of asking many questions in a situation in which there was no negative reaction to irrelevant or stupid questions.

5. PROJECTED NEW COLLEGES STRUCTURES.

We have considered two extreme ways for the restructuring of teaching methods in colleges. First, there is the obvious one of simply extending the method to all of the first-year courses to which the method or a development of the method can be applied. If the method works, then the students will have a better start in each subject. And there will be mutual reinforcement of new habits of thinking and a reorientation toward the activities and problem-solving involved in each subject.

Second, there would be an approach which uses the method in an inclusive course of study which, as we now state it, would branch into various disciplines. To give a concrete example whose focus is mainly social sciences, consider the economics course centering on land reform in Mexico. At a relatively early point in this course, the problem of the legal aspects arises naturally. At that point a lawyer or a law professor (who has been sitting through all class meetings up to that point) is introduced by the economist, who tells the class that normally he has to shut off the discussion of legal aspects because he knows nothing about it except as a layman. However, Professor X teaches law, and the class will henceforth meet with him several hours per week to develop the way in which the lawyers go about handling the problems raised by the land-reform question. In this law class, students will develop the outlook and principles of law, using these legal problems as the focus for class attention in a way entirely similar to the way economic insights were being developed by focusing on land reform. As can readily be imagined, there will also emerge aspects permitting the class to involve political science, sociology, anthropology, history, philosophy, and probably agronomy and even genetics.

This economics class would initially meet 3 or 4 hours per day, 3 or 4 days per week, but would reduce the number of hours as the class started to meet with instructors from other branch subjects.

This approach involves the development of teams of instructors who work out a program for a class of about 25 students. The students would presumably take classes in humanities and languages separately from this single social science course because we have not yet developed any suggestions as to how to handle humanities and languages in the framework of the research studies approach. Each instructor could well be part of several teams, since the period of working with any one team could be anywhere from perhaps one month to four months.

The subjects for each team would seem to be mainly the social sciences, but it is possible to envisage some science or engineering teams. Discussions within a projected team for social sciences at Brandeis University have led to the conjecture that this team activity should last for somewhat less than the first two years of the university program. It is hoped that while students are going through these branched programs they will be exposed to sufficiently different kinds of activities in various subjects to enable them to construct whole areas, if not necessarily individual subjects, in which they will thenceforth concentrate their studies. This approach shows students the nature of activities in various intellectual disciplines as they apply to problems of society. It may reduce the distance between classroom and society and thereby begin to satisfy the demand for "relevance" of college studies in a framework that combines social problems with the integrity of the study of academic disciplines so that both these aspects of student life are enhanced.

CHAPTER VII

Summary and Perspectives

A. SUMMARY

In devising a strategy for education, consideration of the results of our experiments give support to the following assertions.

1. Experience-based learning can appreciably relieve the repression that society and school have placed on the functioning of the curiosity and the motivation to learn in most young people.

2. Experience-based learning is effective to the extent to which it concentrates on the technical and tactical activities involved rather than on the information obtained in any work described.

3. Experience-based learning can work most of its effects in no more than one school term.

4. A large fraction of instructors can handle such courses successfully.

5. Students who have completed one such course can take in information appreciably more rapidly than students taking traditional courses.

6. The more successful experience-based learning course rests firmly on the principle of applying no pressure on students to study; that is, the result of zero pressure is much more than the usual work and study by the vast majority of the students.

7. The successful courses are characterized by very high attendance, very great student participation, and honor grades are attained by most of the students.

If these assertions are accepted as having a large degree of validity, it becomes possible to plan an experiment in college education which should have a fair probability of success. Before making such a plan it is important to deal with the problem of how to know that any such experiment is successful.

Experimentation with new methods in education should be judged in terms of the goals of the education. Unfortunately, there is no general agreement on the goals, because there are several kinds of goals which seem reasonable to most adults and there is no general agreement on the relative emphasis. Furthermore, even if goals were to be agreed upon, our grasp of the social sciences is not great enough for us to know with any degree of sureness how to develop a strategy for achieving those goals. Therefore, in my opinion, most debates about the nature of education in our society are pointless.

Because of this uncertain situation, it would appear to be beyond our hope to say anything worthwhile about evaluating the results of experiments in education. It will then be surprising if I assert that we can characterize a successful experiment—from the teaching and the learning point of view—without making any judgment of the goals or the extent to which those goals are achieved. The support for this statement comes from expanding the analysis begun in Chapter II in which it was asserted that no new course should be considered successful unless most of the students had achieved good grades i.e., a fairly complete understanding of the subject. This theoretical assertion can be compared with the results of teaching many sections by the research studies method. In all sections, the instructors have found that more than a majority of students receive honor grades (i.e. A or B). This has been found for the courses in biology, economics, and chemistry. Thus, there is substantial support to the assertion that the new courses have achieved some fundamentally better results. Analysis of the results of the economics courses permits still further support to be deduced.

In the courses given at Northeastern University, the 15 students in the special section were given the same final examination as the 450 who remained in the regular course. It is not to be expected that the special section covered all of the material of the regular course, although the instructor claimed a substantial overlap. Nevertheless, the numerical results are such as to repay further analysis. A little bit of probability theory will let us get to the heart of the matter.

The students taking the regular course had grades ranging from 40 to 92, with an average of 66. The so-called standard deviation of the average can be approximated by the square root of the average: that is, the square root of 66 which is about 8. Probability theory tells us that two-thirds of the students will receive grades lying between $66-8$ and 66 plus 8; that is, between 58 and 74. This will be true of grades whose major source is the result of random connections between the students and what they learned. It is also shown by probability analysis that a range of plus-or-minus two standard deviations encompasses 95 out of 100 students, and plus-or-minus three standard deviations will encompass about 399 out of 400 students. That is, to use the example of three standard deviations ($3 \times 8 = 24$), marks should range from $66-24$ to 66 plus 24, or between 42 and 90. The theoretical prediction is borne out well by the data for the 450 students whose grades ranged between 40 and 92. Thus, entirely random factors seem to determine the grades of the students. This finding is enough by itself to condemn the regular course; there is not the slightest trace of good teaching, good methodology, or good learning. If there were a truly good teaching-learning situation, all students would have made some substantial achievement so that grades would be less than randomly spread.

The data for the 15 students of the special section can be analyzed in the same way. The average of 68 yields about the same standard deviation of eight. Thus, one-third of the students should receive grades outside the range of 68 minus 8 and 68 plus 8 or between 60 and 76. In fact, none of these students had grades outside the range. Another way of stating this result is that all of these students did about equally well on the standard examination. That is, they *all* studied and mastered at least 60 per cent of the material in the regular course while studying something else. Further, it can be supposed that the major reason these students averaged no more than the regular course students was that some 30 per cent of the material was not covered at all. This indicates then that all the students of the special section learned almost everything set before them. This conclusion was implied by the instructor's remark in his report to his department: "The retention rate . . . of the students appeared far superior to that of a regular principles [of economics] course."

This digression concerning the results of an economics course taught by the research studies method is meant to illustrate the results to be expected of a successful experiment in teaching. It can be known to have been successful if a large majority of the students receive honor grades. In no sense does the obtaining of the result imply that the goals of the experiment were desirable; it means only that the students mastered rather well almost all of the materials studied in such a course. Thus, as maintained at the beginning of this section, it is possible to characterize a successful experiment without making any judgment of the goals or the extent to which the goals were achieved.

This criterion makes it possible to evaluate educational experiments in colleges because even in the United States only about one-third of college-age people are in college; therefore we can expect primarily superior students with superior results. In countries with a much smaller fraction in college, the intellectual quality of the students may be expected to be more homogeneous and, on the average, higher than in the United States.

It is also possible to use this criterion in high schools even in countries which enroll the majority of its youth (where only the "elite" goes to high school, the applicability is similar to that in the college level). It is only necessary to study the results of experiments for those who are, by some reasonable criterion, among the intellectual "elite." A plausible way to characterize the superior students would be, for example, I.Q. scores.

Having given the criterion for evaluating the results of a teaching experiment, we can now turn to devising an experiment in education based on the results of the research studies method. The simplest experiment would be to give first-year college students an entire first-term program of research studies method courses followed, in the second term, by courses which use the combined lecture-research papers framework as presented in Chapter VI. If the experiment works, then virtually all students should receive honor grades during the entire academic year. It would be worthwhile to have a comparison group which followed a standard first-term program before entering the same second-term program. Not having learned how to structure their knowledge, the comparison group students are likely to receive the normal spectrum of grades. However, by the criterion we have proposed, the comparison should not be needed except to confirm our trust in the criterion.

In an empiricist orientation such as has been set forth in these pages, it is not wise to propose the next experiments to be undertaken with such a group, since its nature will depend entirely on the results actually obtained.

B. PERSPECTIVES

Empiricism in education is concerned with both the content and the manner in which young people take in the experience and insights of the present older generation in order to be able to transcend the older generation and hand on a more highly developed culture to their own children. In an earlier chapter it was argued that curriculum-development projects, however badly they are needed—and they *are* badly needed—seem not to be the *most* badly needed educational projects simply because a decade of obviously effective work has yielded little visible alteration in the over-all educational scene. It seems likely that the most pressing current need is for developments in the methodology of education, and such projects should be the focal point for changes in education for the next decade.

This situation seems to have developed because our society has thoughtlessly perpetuated the methodologies of schooling in earlier centuries in today's educational institutions. It could have succeeded, but in fact it did not. Therefore, we are, in effect, using horse-and-buggy educational methods in the jet age. The result is that our society early erodes the curiosity and motivation of most students to the point that curriculum developments benefit only those whose motivation is so great that it survives the deadening effects of present-day social, political, and educational systems.

We are currently in an emergency situation in which the capacity for world-wide communication and annihilation has been developed and handed to a society in which most people are ignorant of or else alienated from human culture, especially that part of human culture we call science. Those of us interested in and involved in the great adventure of human cultural evolution are in great danger of being buried by an avalanche of human goats heedlessly eating the carefully nurtured flowers of human culture and capable of destroying so much that our planet will be turned into a desert in which the very seeds of culture will perish.

In this emergency, experiments in the field of education should concentrate on finding empirically successful ways of releasing the curiosity and motivation of young people. There will be time later to find out what theoretical insights we have gained and to develop theoretical ways of updating the contents of school programs. The relevant consequences of our own experimentation could be summarized by saying that you can't teach anyone anything until his abstractive capacity has been developed; up to that point you can only help him to learn. But, the abilities of young minds to learn and to become active have been grossly underestimated. Indeed, it seems very likely that students can learn anything if their teachers have total faith in their ability to learn.

Appendix 1

In order to indicate how a biology class is conducted, this appendix gives a reconstruction of the study of the classic paper by Emory L. Ellis and Max Delbrück entitled "The Growth of Bacteriophage." The paper is reproduced *in toto* and is followed by the presentation of what has actually occurred in my use of it. This was the first paper studied in my class when I offered a course on the DNA basis of heredity. Appendix II gives the list of papers used for that purpose. (Currently, I use a brief note by d'Herelle before the Ellis-Delbrück paper.)

THE GROWTH OF BACTERIOPHAGE

By EMORY L. ELLIS AND MAX DELBRÜCK*

(*From the William G. Kerckhoff Laboratories of the Biological Sciences, California Institute of Technology, Pasadena*)

(Accepted for publication, September 7, 1938)

INTRODUCTION

Certain large protein molecules (viruses) possess the property of multiplying within living organisms. This process, which is at once so foreign to chemistry and so fundamental to biology, is exemplified in the multiplication of bacteriophage in the presence of susceptible bacteria.

Bacteriophage offers a number of advantages for the study of the multiplication process not available with viruses which multiply at the expense of more complex hosts. It can be stored indefinitely in the absence of a host without deterioration. Its concentration can be determined with fair accuracy by several methods, and even the individual particles can be counted by d'Herelle's method. It can be concentrated, purified, and generally handled like nucleoprotein, to which class of substances it apparently belongs (Schlesinger (1) and Northrop (2)). The host organism is easy to culture and in some cases can be grown in purely synthetic media, thus the conditions of growth of the host and of the phage can be controlled and varied in a quantitative and chemically well defined way.

Before the main problem, which is elucidation of the multiplication process, can be studied, certain information regarding the behavior of phage is needed. Above all, the "natural history" of bacteriophage, *i.e.* its growth under a well defined set of cultural conditions, is as yet insufficiently known, the only extensive quantitative work being that of Krueger and Northrop (3) on an anti-*staphylococcus* phage. The present work is a study of this problem, the growth of another phage (anti-*Escherichia coli* phage) under a standardized set of culture conditions.

* Fellow of The Rockefeller Foundation.

EXPERIMENTAL

Bacteria Culture.—Our host organism was a strain of *Escherichia coli*, which was kindly provided by Dr. C. C. Lindegren. Difco nutrient broth (pH 6.6–6.8) and nutrient agar were selected as culture media. These media were selected for the present work because of the complications which arise when synthetic media are used. We thus avoided the difficulties arising from the need for accessory growth factors.

Isolation, Culture, and Storage of Phage.—A bacteriophage active against this strain of *coli* was isolated in the usual way from fresh sewage filtrates. Its homogeneity was assured by five successive single plaque isolations. The properties of this phage remained constant throughout the work. The average plaque size on 1.5 per cent agar medium was 0.5 to 1.0 mm.

Phage was prepared by adding to 25 cc. of broth, 0.1 cc. of a 20 hour culture of bacteria, and 0.1 cc. of a previous phage preparation. After $3\frac{1}{2}$ hours at 37° the culture had become clear, and contained about 10^9 phage particles.

Such lysates even though stored in the ice box, decreased in phage concentration to about 20 per cent of their initial value in 1 day, and to about 2 per cent in a week, after which they remained constant. Part of this lost phage activity was found to be present in a small quantity of a precipitate which had sedimented during this storage period.

Therefore, lysates were always filtered through Jena sintered glass filters (5 on 3 grade) immediately after preparation. The phage concentration of these filtrates also decreased on storage, though more slowly, falling to 20 per cent in a week. However, 1:100 dilutions in distilled water of the fresh filtered lysates retained a constant assay value for several months, and these diluted preparations were used in the work reported here, except where otherwise specified.

This inactivation of our undiluted filtered phage suspensions on standing is probably a result of a combination of phage and specific phage inhibiting substances from the bacteria, as suggested by Burnett (4, 5). To test this hypothesis we prepared a polysaccharide fraction from agar cultures of these bacteria, according to a method reported by Heidelberger *et al.* (6). Aqueous solutions of this material, when mixed with phage suspensions, rapidly inactivated the phage.

Method of Assay.—We have used a modification of the plaque counting method of d'Herelle (7) throughout this work for the determination of phage concentrations. Although the plaque counting method has been reported unsatisfactory by various investigators, under our conditions it has proven to be entirely satisfactory.

Phage preparations suitably diluted in 18 hour broth cultures of bacteria to give a readily countable number of plaques (100 to 1000) were spread with a bent glass capillary over the surface of nutrient agar plates which had been dried by inverting on sterile filter paper overnight. The plates were then incubated 6 to 24 hours at 37°C. at which time the plaques were readily distinguishable. The 0.1 cc. used for spreading was completely soaked into the agar thus prepared in

366

2 to 3 minutes, thus giving no opportunity for the multiplication of phage in the liquid phase. Each step of each dilution was done with fresh sterile glassware. Tests of the amount of phage adhering to the glass spreaders showed that this quantity is negligible.

The time of contact between phage and bacteria in the final dilution before plating has no measurable influence on the plaque count, up to 5 minutes at 25°C. Even if phage alone is spread on the plate and allowed to soak in for 10 minutes, before seeding the plate with bacteria, only a small decrease in plaque count is apparent (about 20 per cent). This decrease we attribute to failure of some phage particles to come into contact with bacteria.

Under parallel conditions, the reproducibility of an assay is limited by the sampling error, which in this case is equal to the square root of the number of plaques (10 per cent for counts of 100; 3.2 per cent for counts of 1000). To test the effect of phage concentration on the number of plaques obtained, successive dilutions of a phage preparation were all plated, and the number of plaques enumerated. Over a 100-fold range of dilution, the plaque count was in linear proportion to the phage concentration. (See Fig. 1.)

Dreyer and Campbell-Renton (8) using a different anti-*coli* phage and an anti-*staphylococcus* phage, and a different technique found a complicated dependence of plaque count on dilution. Such a finding is incompatible with the concept that phage particles behave as single particles, *i.e.* without interaction, with respect to plaque formation. Our experiments showed no evidence of such a complicated behavior, and we ascribe it therefore to some secondary cause inherent in their procedure.

Bronfenbrenner and Korb (9) using a phage active against *B. dysenteriae* Shiga, and a different plating technique found that when the agar concentration was changed from 1 per cent to 2.5 per cent, the number of plaques was reduced to 1 per cent of its former value. They ascribed this to a change in the water supplied to the bacteria. With the technique which we have employed, variation of the agar concentration from 0.75 per cent to 3.0 per cent, had little influence on the number of plaques produced, though the size decreased noticeably with increasing agar concentration. (See Table I.)

Changes in the concentration of bacteria spread with the phage on the agar plates had no important influence on the number of plaques obtained. (See Table I.) The temperature at which plates were incubated had no significant effect on the number of plaques produced. (See Table I.)

In appraising the accuracy of this method, several points must be borne in mind. With our phage, our experiments confirm in the main the picture proposed by d'Herelle, according to which a phage particle grows in the following way: it becomes attached to a susceptible bacterium, multiplies upon or within it up to a critical time, when the newly formed phage particles are dispersed into the solution.

In the plaque counting method a single phage particle and an infected bacterium containing any number of phage particles will each give only one plaque.

367

This method therefore, does not give the number of phage particles but the number of loci within the solution at which one or more phage particles exist. These loci will hereafter be called "infective centers." The linear relationship between phage concentration and plaque count (Fig. 1) does not prove that the number of plaques is equal to the number of infective centers, but only that it is proportional to this number. We shall call the fraction of infective centers which

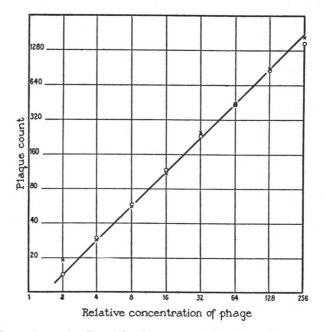

FIG. 1. Proportionality of the phage concentration to the plaque count.

Successive twofold dilutions of a phage preparation were plated in duplicate on nutrient agar; 0.1 cc. on each plate. The plaque counts from two such series of dilutions are plotted against the relative phage concentration, both on a logarithmic scale.

produces plaques the "efficiency of plating." With the concentrations of phage and bacteria which we have used this coefficient is essentially the fraction of infected bacteria in the suspension spread on the plate, which goes through to lysis under our cultural conditions on the agar medium. After plating, the phage particles released by this lysis infect the surrounding bacteria, increasing only the size, and not the number of plaques.

TABLE I

Independence of Plaque Count on Plating Method

Agar concentration

Plates were prepared in which the agar strength varied, and all spread with 0.1 cc. of the same dilution of a phage preparation. There is no significant difference in the numbers of plaques obtained.

Agar concentration, *per cent*	0.75	1.5	3.0
Plaque counts	394	373	424
	408	430	427
	376	443	455
	411	465	416
	373	404	469
Average	392	423	438
Plaque size, *mm*	2	0.5	0.2

Concentration of plating *coli*

A broth suspension of bacteria (10^9 bacteria/cc.) was prepared from a 24 hour agar slant and used at various dilutions, as the plating suspension for a single phage dilution. There are no significant differences in the plaque counts except at the highest dilution of the bacterial suspension, where the count is about 15 per cent lower.

Concentration	Plaque count
1	920
1/5	961
1/25	854
1/125	773

Temperature of plate incubation

Twelve plates were spread with 0.1 cc. of the same suspension of phage and bacteria, divided into three groups, and incubated at different temperatures. There were no significant differences in the plaque counts obtained.

Temperature, °C	37	24	10
Plaque count	352	384	405
	343	405	377
	386	403	400
	422	479	406
Average	376	418	397

The experimental determination of the efficiency of plating is described in a later section (see p. 379). The coefficient varies from 0.3 to 0.5. This means that three to five out of every ten infected bacteria produce plaques. The fact that the efficiency of plating is relatively insensitive to variations in the temperature of plate incubation, density of plating *coli*, concentration of agar, etc. indicates that a definite fraction of the infected bacteria in the broth cultures do not readily go through to lysis when transferred to agar plates. For most experiments only the relative assay is significant; we have therefore, given the values derived directly from the plaque counts without taking into account the efficiency of plating, unless the contrary is stated.

Growth Measurements

The main features of the growth of this phage in broth cultures of the host are shown in Fig. 2. After a small initial increase (discussed below) the number of infective centers (individual phage particles, plus infected bacteria) in the suspension remains constant for a time, then rises sharply to a new value, after which it again remains constant. Later, a second sharp rise, not as clear-cut as the first, and finally a third rise occur. At this time visible lysis of the bacterial suspension takes place. A number of features of the growth process may be deduced from this and similar experiments, and this is the main concern of the present paper.

The Initial Rise

When a concentration of phage suitable for plating was added to a suspension of bacteria, and plated at once, a reproducible plaque count was obtained. If the suspension with added phage was allowed to stand 5 minutes at 37°C. (or 20 minutes at 25°C.) the number of plaques obtained on plating the suspension was found to be 1.6 times higher. This initial rise is not to be confused with the first "burst" which occurs later and increases the plaque count 70-fold. After the initial rise, the new value is readily duplicated and remains constant until the start of the first burst in the growth curve (30 minutes at 37° and 60 minutes at 25°).

This initial rise we attribute not to an increase in the number of infective centers, but to an increase in the probability of plaque formation (*i.e.* an increase in the efficiency of plating) by infected bacteria in a progressed state; that is, bacteria in which the phage particle has commenced to multiply. That this rise results from a change in the

370

efficiency of plating and not from a quick increase in the number of infective centers is evident from the following experiment. Bacteria were grown for 24 hours at 25°C. on agar slants, then suspended in broth. Phage was added to this suspension and to a suspension of bacteria grown in the usual way, and the concentration of infective

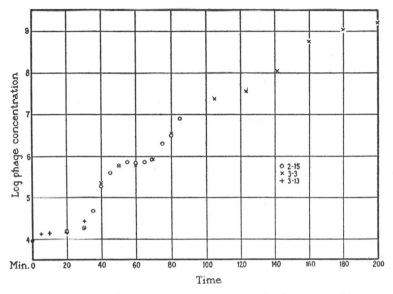

FIG. 2. Growth of phage in the presence of growing bacteria at 37°C.

A diluted phage preparation was mixed with a suspension of bacteria containing 2×10^8 organisms per cc., and diluted after 3 minutes 1 to 50 in broth. At this time about 70 per cent of the phage had become attached to bacteria. The total number of infective centers was determined at intervals on samples of this growth mixture. Three such experiments, done on different days, are plotted in this figure. The same curve was easily reproducible with all phage preparations stored under proper conditions.

centers was determined on both. The initial value was 1.6 times higher in the agar grown bacteria than in the control experiment, and remained constant until actual growth occurred. The initial rise was therefore absent in this case, clearly a result of an increase in the efficiency of plating. A sufficient number of experiments were performed with bacteria grown on agar to indicate that in other respects their behavior is similar to that of the bacteria grown in broth.   The bacteria grown in this way on agar slants are in some way more susceptible to lysis than the broth cultured bacteria.

Adsorption

The first step in the growth of bacteriophage is its attachment to susceptible bacteria.   The rate of this attachment can be readily measured by centrifuging the bacteria out of a suspension containing phage, at various times, and determining the amount of phage which remains unattached in the supernatant (*cf.* Krueger (10)).[1]

According to the picture of phage growth outlined above, phage cannot multiply except when attached to bacteria; therefore, the rate of attachment may, under certain conditions, limit the rate of growth. We wished to determine the rate of this adsorption so that it could be taken into account in the interpretation of growth experiments, or eliminated if possible, as a factor influencing the growth rate.   Our growth curves show that there is no increase in the number of infective centers up to a critical time; we could therefore, make measurements of the adsorption on living bacteria suspended in broth, so long as the time allowed for attachment was less than the time to the start of the first burst in the growth curve.   The adsorption proved to be so rapid that this time interval was ample to obtain adsorption of all but a few per cent of the free phage if the bacteria concentration was above 3×10^7.   The number of bacteria remained constant; the lag phase in their growth was longer than the experimental period.

The rate of attachment was found to be first order with respect to the concentration of free phage (P_f) and first order with respect to the concentration of bacteria (B) over a wide range of concentrations, in agreement with the results reported by Krueger (10).   That is, the concentration of free phage followed the equation

$$- \frac{d(P_f)}{dt} = k_a(P_f)(B)$$

[1] A very careful study of the adsorption of a *coli*-phage has also been made by Schlesinger (Schlesinger, M., *Z. Hyg. u. Infektionskrankh.*, 1932, **114**, 136, 149).   Our results, which are less accurate and complete, agree qualitatively and quantitatively with the results of his detailed studies.

in which k_a was found to be 1.2×10^{-9} cm.^{3}/min. at 15° and 1.9×10^{-9} cm.^{3}/min. at 25°C. These rate constants are about five times greater than those reported by Krueger (10). With our ordinary 18 hour bacteria cultures (containing 2×10^8 *B. coli*/cc.) we thus obtain 70 per cent attachment of phage in 3 minutes and 98 per cent in 10 minutes. The adsorption follows the equation accurately until more than 90 per cent attachment has been accomplished, and then slows down somewhat, indicating either that not all the phage particles have the same affinity for the bacteria, or that equilibrium is being approached. Other experiments not recorded here suggest that, if an equilibrium exists, it lies too far in favor of adsorption to be readily detected. This equation expresses the rate of adsorption even when a tenfold excess of phage over bacteria is present, indicating that a single bacterium can accommodate a large number of phage particles on its surface, as found by several previous workers (5, 10).

Krueger (10) found a true equilibrium between free and adsorbed phage. The absence of a detectable desorption in our case may result from the fixation of adsorbed phage by growth processes, since our conditions permitted growth, whereas Krueger's experiments were conducted at a temperature at which the phage could not grow.

Growth of Phage

Following adsorption of the phage particle on a susceptible bacterium, multiplication occurs, though this is not apparent as an increase in the number of plaques until the bacterium releases the resulting colony of phage particles into the solution. Because the adsorption under proper conditions is so rapid and complete (as shown above) experiments could be devised in which only the influence of the processes following adsorption could be observed.

The details of these experiments were as follows: 0.1 cc. of a phage suspension of appropriate concentration was added to 0.9 cc. of an 18 hour broth bacterial culture, containing about 2×10^8 *B. coli* / cc. After standing for a few minutes, 70 to 90 per cent of the phage was attached to the bacteria. At this time, the mixture was diluted 50-fold in broth (previously adjusted to the required temperature) and incubated. Samples were removed at regular intervals, and the concentration of infective centers determined.

373

The results of three experiments at 37°C. are plotted in Fig. 2, and confirm the suggestion of d'Herelle that phage multiplies under a spatial constraint, *i.e.* within or upon the bacterium, and is suddenly liberated in a burst. It is seen that after the initial rise (discussed above) the count of infective centers remains constant up to 30 minutes, and then rises about 70-fold above the initial value. The rise corresponds to the liberation of the phage particles which have multiplied in the initial constant period. This interpretation was verified by measurements of the free phage by centrifuging out the infected bacteria, and determining the number of phage particles in the supernatant liquid. The free phage concentration after adsorption was, of course, small compared to the total and remained constant up to the time of the first rise. It then rose steeply and became substantially equal to the total phage.

The number of bacteria lysed in this first burst is too small a fraction of the total bacteria used in these experiments to be measured as a change in turbidity; the ratio of uninfected bacteria to the total possible number of infected bacteria before the first burst is 400 to 1, the largest number of bacteria which can disappear in the first burst is therefore only 0.25 per cent of the total.

The phage particles liberated in the first burst are free to infect more bacteria. These phage particles then multiply within or on the newly infected bacteria; nevertheless, as before, the concentration of infective centers remains constant until these bacteria are lysed and release the phage which they contain into the medium. This gives the second burst which begins at about 70 minutes from the start of the experiment. Since the uninfected bacteria have been growing during this time, the bacteria lysed in the second burst amount to less than 5 per cent of the total bacteria present at this time. There is again therefore, no visible lysis.

This process is repeated, leading to a third rise of smaller magnitude starting at 120 minutes. At this time, inspection of the culture, which has until now been growing more turbid with the growth of the uninfected bacteria, shows a rapid lysis. The number of phage particles available at the end of the second rise was sufficient to infect the remainder of the bacteria.

These results are typical of a large number of such experiments, at

374

37°, all of which gave the 70-fold burst size, *i.e.* an average of 70 phage particles per infected bacterium, occurring quite accurately at the time shown, 30 minutes. Indeed, one of the most striking features of these experiments was the constancy of the time interval from adsorption to the start of the first burst. The magnitude of the rise (70-fold) was likewise readily reproducible by all phage preparations which had been stored under proper conditions to prevent deterioration (see above).

Multiple Infection

The adsorption measurements showed that a single bacterium can adsorb many phage particles. The subsequent growth of phage in these "multiple infected" bacteria might conceivably lead to (*a*) an increase in burst size; (*b*) a burst at an earlier time, or (*c*) the same burst size at the same time, as if only one of the adsorbed particles had been effective, and the others inactivated. In the presence of very great excesses of phage, Krueger and Northrop (3) and Northrop (2) report that visible lysis of the bacteria occurs in a very short time. It was possible therefore, that in our case, the latent period could be shortened by multiple infection. To determine this point, we have made several experiments of which the following is an example. 0.8 cc. of a freshly prepared phage suspension containing 4×10^9 particles per cc. (assay corrected for efficiency of plating) was added to 0.2 cc. of bacterial suspension containing 4×10^9 bacteria per cc. The ratio of phage to bacteria in this mixture was 4 to 1. 5 minutes were allowed for adsorption, and then the mixture was diluted 1 to 12,500 in broth, incubated at 25°, and the growth of the phage followed by plating at 20 minute intervals, with a control growth curve in which the phage to bacteria ratio was 1 to 10. No significant difference was found either in the latent period or in the size of the burst. The bacteria which had adsorbed several phage particles behaved as if only one of these particles was effective.

Effect of Temperature on Latent Period and Burst Size

A change in temperature might change either the latent period, *i.e.* the time of the burst, or change the size of the burst, or both. In order to obtain more accurate estimates of the burst size it is desirable

375

to minimize reinfection during the period of observation.   This is obtained by diluting the phage-bacteria mixture (after initial contact to secure adsorption) to such an extent that the rate of adsorption then becomes extremely small.   In this way, a single "cycle" of growth, (infection, growth, burst) was obtained as the following example

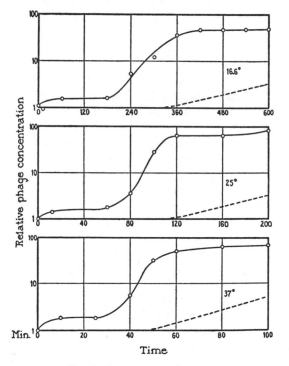

FIG. 3. One-step growth curves.

A suitable dilution of phage was mixed with a suspension of bacteria containing 2×10^8 organisms per cc. and allowed to stand at the indicated temperature for 10 minutes to obtain more than 90 per cent adsorption of the phage. This mixture was then diluted $1:10^4$ in broth, and incubated.   It was again diluted $1:10$ at the start of the first rise to further decrease the rate of adsorption of the phage set free in the first step.   The time scales are in the ratio 1:2:6 for the temperatures 37, 25, and 16.6°C.   Log P/P_0 is plotted, P_0 being the initial concentration of infective centers and P the concentration at time t.   The broken line indicates the growth curve of the bacteria under the corresponding conditions.

376

shows.   0.1 cc. of phage of appropriate and known concentration was added to 0.9 cc. of an 18 hour culture and allowed to stand in this concentrated bacterial suspension for 10 minutes at the temperature of the experiment.   This mixture was then diluted $1:10^4$ in broth and incubated at the temperature chosen.   Samples of this diluted mixture were withdrawn at regular intervals and assayed.   The results of three such experiments are plotted in Fig. 3.   The rise corresponds to the average number of phage produced per burst, and its value can be appraised better in these experiments than in the complete growth curve previously given (Fig. 2) where there is probably some overlapping of the steps.   In these experiments the rise is seen to be practically identical at the three temperatures, and equals about sixty particles per infected bacterium, but the time at which the rise occurred was 30 minutes at 37°, 60 minutes at 25°, and 180 minutes at 16.6°.   This shows that the effect of temperature is solely on the latent period.

We have also made separate measurements of the rate of bacterial growth under the conditions of these experiments.   They show that the average division period of the bacteria in their logarithmic growth phase varies in the same way with temperature, as the length of the latent period of phage growth.   The figures are:

Temperature	Division period of *B*	Latent period of *P* growth
°C	*min.*	*min.*
16.6	About 120	180
25	42	60
37	21	30

There is a constant ratio (3/2) between the latent period of phage growth and the division period of the bacteria.   This coincidence suggests a connection between the time required for division of a bacterium under optimum growth conditions, and the time from its infection by phage to its lysis.

Individual Phage Particle

The growth curves described above give averages only of large numbers of bursts.   They can, however, also be studied individually, as was first done by Burnett (11).

377

If from a mixture containing many particles very small samples are withdrawn, containing each on the average only about one or less particles, then the fraction p_r of samples containing r particles is given by Poissons' (12) formula,

$$p_r = \frac{n^r e^{-n}}{r!} \tag{1}$$

where n is the average number of particles in a sample and e is the Napierian logarithm base.   If the average number n is unknown, it can be evaluated from an experimental determination of any single

TABLE II

Distribution of Individual Particles among Small Samples

A suitably diluted phage preparation was added to 5 cc. of 18 hour bacteria culture and 0.1 cc. samples of this mixture were plated.   The distribution of particles among the samples is that predicted by formula (1).

	p_r (experimental)	p_r (calculated)
0 plaques on 13 plates	0.394	0.441
1 plaque " 14 "	0.424	0.363
2 plaques " 5 "	0.151	0.148
3 " " 1 plate	0.033	0.040
4 " " 0 plates	0.000	0.008
27 " " 33 "	1.002	1.000

one of the p_r, for instance from a determination of p_0, the fraction of samples containing no particles:

$$n = -\ln p_0 \tag{2}$$

Let us now consider the following experiment.   A small number of phage particles is added to a suspension containing bacteria in high concentration.   Within a few minutes each phage particle has attached itself to a bacterium.   The mixture is then diluted with a large volume of broth, in order to have the bacteria in low concentration so that after the first burst a long time elapses before reinfection, as in the one step growth curves.   Samples (0.05 cc.) are removed from this mixture to separate small vials and incubated at the desired temperature.   If these samples are plated separately (after adding a drop of bacterial suspension to each vial) before the occurrence of bursts, the fraction of the plates containing 0, 1, 2, *etc*. plaques is found

378

to conform to formula (1) (see Table II). In this experiment we could also have inferred the average number of particles per sample, using formula (2), from the fraction of the plates showing no plaques (giving 0.93 per sample) instead of from the total number of plaques $(27/33 = 0.82$ per sample).

Experimental Measure of Efficiency of Plating

If the samples are incubated until the bursts have occurred, and then plated, the samples which had no particles will still show no plaques, those with one or more particles will show a large number, depending on the size of the burst, and on the efficiency of plating. In any case, if we wait until all bursts have occurred, only those samples which really contained no particle will show no plaques, quite independent of any inefficiency of plating. From this fraction of plates showing no plaques we can therefore evaluate the true number of particles originally present in the solution, and by comparison with the regular assay evaluate the efficiency of plating. In this way we have determined our efficiency of plating to be about 0.4. For instance, one such experiment gave no plaques on 23 out of 40 plates, and many plaques on each of the remaining plates. This gives $p_0 = \dfrac{23}{40}$ or 0.57 from which $n = 0.56$ particles per sample. A parallel assay of the stock phage used indicated 0.22 particles per sample; the plating efficiency was therefore $\dfrac{0.22}{0.56} = 0.39$. This plating efficiency remains fairly constant under our standard conditions for assay. The increase in probability of plaque formation which we suppose to take place following the infection of a bacterium by the phage particle, *i.e.* the initial rise, brings the plating efficiency up to 0.65.

The Burst Size

Single particle experiments such as that described above, revealed a great fluctuation in the magnitude of individual bursts, far larger than one would expect from the differences in size of the individual bacteria in a culture; indeed, they vary from a few particles to two hundred or more. Data from one such experiment are given in Table III.

379

98 A STRATEGY FOR EDUCATION

We at first suspected that the fluctuation in burst size was connected with the time of the burst, in that early bursts were small and late bursts big, and the fluctuation was due to the experimental superposition of these. However, measurement of a large number of bursts, plated at a time when only a small fraction of the bursts had occurred, showed the same large fluctuation. We then suspected that the particles of a burst were not liberated simultaneously, but over an interval of time. In this case one might expect a greater homogeneity

TABLE III

Fluctuation in Individual Burst Size

97.9 per cent of phage attached to bacteria in presence of excess bacteria (10 minutes), this mixture diluted, and samples incubated 200 minutes, then entire sample plated with added bacteria.

	Bursts
25 plates show 0 plaques	
1 plate shows 1 plaque	
14 plates show bursts	130
Average burst size, taking account of probable doubles = 48	58
	26
	123
	83
	9
	31
	5
	53
	48
	72
	45
	190
	9
Total..	882 plaques

in burst size, if measurements were made at a late time when they are at their maximum value. This view also was found by experiment to be false.

The cause of the great fluctuation in burst size is therefore still obscure.

DISCUSSION

The results presented above show that the growth of this strain of phage is not uniform, but in bursts. These bursts though of constant

380

average size, under our conditions, vary widely in individual size. A burst occurs after a definite latent period following the adsorption of the phage on susceptible bacteria, and visible lysis coincides only with the last step-wise rise in the growth curve when the phage particles outnumber the bacteria present. It seemed reasonable to us to assume that the burst is identical with the lysis of the individual bacterium.

Krueger and Northrop (3), in their careful quantitative studies of an anti-*staphylococcus* phage came to an interpretation of their results which differs in some important respects from the above:

1. Their growth curves were smooth and gave no indication of steps; they concluded therefore that the production of phage is a continuous process.

2. In their case, the free phage during the logarithmic phase of a growth curve was an almost constant small fraction of the total phage. This led them to the view that there is an equilibrium between intra-cellular and extracellular phage. With an improved technique, Krueger (10) found that the fraction of free phage decreased in proportion to the growth of the bacteria, in conformity with the assumption of an equilibrium between two phases.

3. Krueger and Northrop (3) found that visible lysis occurred when a critical ratio of total phage to bacteria had been attained, and they assumed that there was no lysis in the earlier period of phage growth.

To appreciate the nature of these differences it must be born in mind that their method of assay was essentially different from ours. They used, as a measure of the "activity" of the sample of phage assayed, the time required for it to lyse a test suspension of bacteria under standard conditions. This time interval, according to the picture of the growth process given here, is the composite effect of a number of factors: the average time required for adsorption of free phage, its rate of growth in the infected bacteria, the time and size of burst, and the average time required for repetition of this process until the number of phage particles exceeds the number of bacteria and infects substantially all of them. Then, after a time interval equal to the latent period, lysis occurs.

This lysis assay method tends to measure the total number of phage particles rather than the number of infective centers as the

381

following considerations show. Let us take a sample of a growth mixture in which is suspended one infected bacterium containing fifty phage particles. If this sample is plated, it can show but a single plaque. However, if the sample is assayed by the lysis method, this single infective center soon sets free its fifty particles (or more, if multiplication is still proceeding) and the time required to attain lysis will approximate that for fifty free particles rather than that for a single particle.

Since the burst does not lead to an increase in the number of phage particles, but only to their dispersion into the solution, the lysis method cannot give any steps in the concentration of the *total* phage in a growth curve. On the other hand one might have expected a step-wise increase in the concentration of *free* phage. However, the adsorption rate of the phage used by Krueger (10) is so slow that the infection of the bacteria is spread over a time longer than the presumed latent period, and therefore the bursts would be similarly spread in time, smoothing out any steps which might otherwise appear. Moreover, their measurements were made at 30 minute intervals, which even in our case would have been insufficient to reveal the steps.

The ratio between intracellular and extracellular phage would be determined, according to this picture of phage growth, by the ratio of the average time of adsorption to the average latent period. The average time of adsorption would decrease as the bacteria increased, shifting the ratio of intracellular to extracellular phage in precisely the manner described by Krueger (10).

As we have indicated in the description of our growth curves, lysis of bacteria should become visible only at a late time. Infection of a large fraction of the bacteria is possible only after the free phage has attained a value comparable to the number of bacteria, and visible lysis should then set in after the lapse of a latent period. At this time the total phage (by activity assay) will be already large compared to the number of bacteria, in agreement with Krueger and Northrop's findings.

It appears therefore that while Krueger and Northrop's picture does not apply to our phage and bacteria, their results do not exclude for their phage the picture which we have adopted. It would be of fundamental importance if two phages behave in such a markedly different way.

SUMMARY

1. An anti-*Escherichia coli* phage has been isolated and its behavior studied.

2. A plaque counting method for this phage is described, and shown to give a number of plaques which is proportional to the phage concentration. The number of plaques is shown to be independent of agar concentration, temperature of plate incubation, and concentration of the suspension of plating bacteria.

3. The efficiency of plating, *i.e.* the probability of plaque formation by a phage particle, depends somewhat on the culture of bacteria used for plating, and averages around 0.4.

4. Methods are described to avoid the inactivation of phage by substances in the fresh lysates.

5. The growth of phage can be divided into three periods: adsorption of the phage on the bacterium, growth upon or within the bacterium (latent period), and the release of the phage (burst).

6. The rate of adsorption of phage was found to be proportional to the concentration of phage and to the concentration of bacteria. The rate constant k_a is 1.2×10^{-9} cm.^{3}/min. at 15°C. and 1.9×10^{-9} cm.^{3}/min. at 25°.

7. The average latent period varies with the temperature in the same way as the division period of the bacteria.

8. The latent period before a burst of individual infected bacteria varies under constant conditions between a minimal value and about twice this value.

9. The average latent period and the average burst size are neither increased nor decreased by a fourfold infection of the bacteria with phage.

10. The average burst size is independent of the temperature, and is about 60 phage particles per bacterium.

11. The individual bursts vary in size from a few particles to about 200. The same variability is found when the early bursts are measured separately, and when all the bursts are measured at a late time.

One of us (E. L. E.) wishes to acknowledge a grant in aid from Mrs. Seeley W. Mudd. Acknowledgment is also made of the assistance of Mr. Dean Nichols during the preliminary phases of the work.

REFERENCES

1. Schlesinger, M., *Biochem. Z.*, Berlin, 1934, **273**, 306.
2. Northrop, J. H., *J. Gen. Physiol.*, 1938, **21**, 335.
3. Krueger, A. P., and Northrop, J. H., *J. Gen. Physiol.*, 1930, **14**, 223.
4. Burnett, F. M., *Brit. J. Exp. Path.*, 1927, **8**, 121.
5. Burnett, F. M., Keogh, E. V., and Lush, D., *Australian J. Exp. Biol. and Med. Sc.*, 1937, **15**, suppl. to part 3, p. 227.
6. Heidelberger, M., Kendall, F. E., and Scherp, H. W., *J. Exp. Med.*, 1936, **64**, 559.
7. d'Herelle, F., The bacteriophage and its behavior, Baltimore, The Williams & Wilkins Co., 1926.
8. Dreyer, C., and Campbell-Renton, M. L., *J. Path. and Bact.*, 1933, **36**, 399.
9. Bronfenbrenner, J. J., and Korb, C., *Proc. Soc. Exp. Biol. and Med.*, 1923, **21**, 315.
10. Krueger, A. P., *J. Gen. Physiol.*, 1931, **14**, 493.
11. Burnett, F. M., *Brit. J. Exp. Path.*, 1929, **10**, 109.
12. Poissons, S. D., Recherches sur la probabilité des jugements en matière criminelle et en matière civile, précédées des règles générales du calcul des probabilités, Paris, 1837.

Obviously, every instructor runs his class in a characteristic way. Indeed, each time a particular paper is used, the sequence of class events differs because the students happen to raise other questions or similar questions in a different way or in a sequence which effects a different train of thoughts in the instructor's mind. Since the emphasis of the course is on experimental activities and not primarily on biological information, it makes little difference if an instructor's spectacularly successful development is bypassed by the next class. It is only important to get the students to put themselves in the place of the experimenters and to ask themselves what they should *do* next.

The Ellis-Delbrück paper is useful because it is readily possible to get students to anticipate some of the next things to be done after having gone over any particular part of the paper. As the first paper, it should be worked on for about three weeks. If only a week or so has been spent on the paper, it will be found that the *information* has been emphasized and not the *activities* involved in obtaining the information. If four or more weeks are taken up it is likely that the students will become bored, inasmuch as they are not learning anything new other than detailed information. The decision about when to leave a paper is made with increasing skill as instructors gain experience with this way of handling classes.

For its first home-study assignment the class is told to skim through the entire paper in ten or twenty minutes just to see its structure and, to a small extent, its content. Then, the first section should be studied for about one hour, noting or underlining every technical term that is not *entirely* understood. These terms should be asked about in class at the next meeting.

It is probably obvious from reading the first page of the paper that the class would ask the meanings of about twenty terms at the next meeting. These are likely to be: growth, bacteriophage, protein, molecule, viruses, organism, susceptible bacteria, complex, hosts, d'Herelle's method, nucleo-protein, culture, synthetic media, anti-staphylococcus phage, anti-*Escherichia coli* phage.

When, as in this instance, it is likely that there will be a long list of terms to explain and define, it is desirable to write the list of terms on the board, as the students ask about them, until some ten or twenty terms are there waiting to be discussed. Since the instructor can guess beforehand what terms will be indicated, he can be prepared to explain them in some way and in some sequence that seems suitable to him. Before giving an example of this, it *must* be stressed again that all explanations should be presented in terms of the *activities* of the experimental scientists who initially explained or defined the terms.

It seems easiest for me to begin by reminding the class of the cell theory of living organisms. Most students will nod readily when the instructor asks if they know the theory that all living organisms are composed of cells. The nods will stop abruptly when the instructor asks how such a theory could be supported experimentally. What, asks the instructor, should you *do* to test the hypothesis that the cell theory is valid? Some students will shortly suggest looking through a microscope. The instructor asks, "At what?" Some object, perhaps human skin, will be suggested. The instructor asks that student if he will be convinced by seeing some oval structures in his skin; will the class also be thereby convinced that *all* organisms are composed *entirely* of cells. Further, is it really true that there is no material in the spaces between cells? How would you find out? What would you *do* to find out?

There is a point at which additional questions can no longer effectively be brought out with the class, and then the instructor needs to supply some answers. The instructor should point out gently that he is then going to show them how to work at such a set of questions and he hopes that the next time, or after the next time, the class will get further by itself.

He then goes on to point out the existence of many microscope studies and of animal and human development from fertilized eggs or other such kinds of experimental evidence. If it seems indicated by the quality of the mood and attentiveness of the class, he can point out the incomplete nature of all replies to all questions. That is, after scientists have looked enough, it is likely that they will take on faith that all the other organisms will also be composed of cells. That doesn't mean, he should point out, that there cannot be other strategies of life. Some of the students may have read Hoyle's *The Black Cloud* in which a very weird form of life is imagined that violates no known biological principles. This point can be tied into some of the scientist's current fascination with space travel because of the opportunity to learn something about the uniqueness of the development of life on our own planet.

The class is asked why Nature has evolved a cell structure for organisms. Then, this question is sharpened to ask what problems the cell has in growing or replicating. The class will eventually suggest such aspects as: (1) The cell has to gather the building blocks for making copies of itself. (2) The cell has to gain energy for doing its work, including the gathering of its building blocks.

At this point the class should be asked to set forth the experimental questions that would permit it to know if energy is needed. That is, one doesn't ask the class if such factors as temperature and nutrient concentration and metabolic poisoning or turning off the air are important; the class has to be helped to think about such questions, however crudely, and then shown that, in fact, these are the correct forms of the questions as we know them today. To achieve the result of getting the class to ask about temperature, etc., you can ask the class to guess the conditions under which cells would grow slowly. The class will come up with . . . cold, lack of nutrients, lack of air, etc. Then, you can ask what should be measured to know if these factors do, indeed, affect cell growth. They will eventually arrive at the idea of measuring the mass or volume of cells if grown in flasks at various temperatures, with various dilutions of nutrients, and with varying amounts of air being blown in. They should then be asked what they would actually measure. Someone will point out that one should collect all the cells and either count them or weigh them. You might want to have them talk about the differences between these two measures of growth—it might even be possible to use the conjecture to evoke consideration of what determines the sizes of cells. Why don't they grow to varying sizes; or, do they? What factors would you need to consider to determine what they do? How would you measure them? It is readily seen that consideration of a single point can branch out to a year's worth of studies if the questions are all to be answered. It is also probably worthwhile to point this out to the class as an illustration of the contention that the answer to any nontrivial question (certainly in science and probably in all fields) will include an understanding of the whole field. That, one can remark, is why the study of biology in a course such as ours can be begun by studying viruses, plants, molds, photosynthesis, shellfish, blood, flies, elephants, or even man himself.

It should be rather obvious that the class will be lost if such a recital is continued very long. At some point you will sense, or be told indignantly, that the class members are becoming confused about the whole trend of the discussion . . . it seems to be leading everywhere and nowhere. It is at that point that you must tell the class that you will have to give it some information and ask permission to talk for five or ten minutes.

My own usual starting point is to draw a sketch of a cell, indicating a membrane, and then a set of rectangles is placed inside and each is labeled as some kind of factory: power, fat, protein, starch, heredity, intake, excretion, etc. After the first one or two have been labeled, the class might be asked to indicate the other labels; the decision about getting the class back into the discussion is an instinctive one for the instructor, who has to sense when students want to be told and when they are ready to do some of the thinking. Remember, too, that students will develop skills in doing this analysis as the term progresses, so it is not necessary to have them achieve very much while studying the first paper. Continuing with the study of the cell, one can then show the class a large electron micrograph and/or a light micrograph of a cell. What would you do now to investigate the cell's structure? Some student will *know* that the oval body in the middle is the nucleus. Experimentally what does he mean by nucleus or is he just using another word for the heredity factory or fat factory? He will identify the nucleus as being connected with heredity. How could that be proved? He will say because it contains the chromosomes on which there are genes determining inheritance. What would you do to verify or to prove or suspect *for the first time* that the assertion is correct? What was the problem faced by the first person who had the idea that nuclei are in some manner associated with inheritance of properties? Maybe you can separate the nuclei from the rest of the cell, a student suggests. If so, you reply, what good would that do you? The silence tends to be broken by someone who points out that you can show that the nucleus contains DNA and that is known to give the inheritable properties. You ask how you would demonstrate that (it is better to turn to the class and ask them what question you will fling back at the student . . . they will frequently have taken the point and will chorus something about how does he know it is connected with heredity). Then I ask the students the name of the course. There will be some fumbling and some remarks like Biology XX. I remind the class that the name is the "DNA basis of heredity." It seems that we are going to spend an entire term developing the reasons why it is believed that DNA has something to do with heredity. At this point I ask if any student knows a single experimental fact that would make him believe that DNA has anything to do with heredity. Most classes contain no such students. One class had a student who mentioned the Hershey-Chase experiment showing independent functions of phage protein and nucleic acid and showing that the nucleic acid fraction of phages could, with small amounts of protein, effect the synthesis of intact and biologically active phages. This class was led to discuss if even this approximate result for phages would necessarily hold for larger and more complex bacteria, nucleated cells, etc. Most classes admit not knowing any evidence. Such classes should be helped to decide what kinds of experimental results could convince them. For example, infecting cells or animals with pure virus DNA and getting normal whole viruses would be rather convincing.

The upshot of all this digression is to demonstrate that there must be experimental bases for generalizations, and the experimental bases normally have incomplete aspects which leave room for doubting the inferences. This is a good point to note something which should be demonstrated several times during the term: that is to distinguish between an experimental result and its interpretation. Here I would just call attention to the point and continue the preceding discussion.

The question of identification is generally continued. Looking at the micrograph of a cell, one can ask where are the various factories we have indicated in our schematic cell. We must ask how to identify any particular organelle with any one or several of the factories. Students can be helped by hints to get at the problem in one of two alternative ways. First, they could try to identify which organelle does what. Second, they could set themselves the task of designing the cell and ask what kind of cell geometry would be needed to accommodate any set of strategies they may have suggested for the cell.

Now, not all of the preceding lines of discussion will be done with any one class, for it will be found that the students will not accept such lengthy digressions, but the instructor who uses these kinds of notions can mark down which he has used and he will find it easy later in the term to raise the other aspects which continue his own peculiar way of thinking about nature.

Thus after several meetings, the class will have worked out some set of problems and strategies for cells. Somewhere in all this I will have set forth a point mentioned in the main text: my indication that every fact of Nature implies two things: a problem that Nature had and a particular solution to that problem. I illustrate it here too.

Having explained the major features of a typical cell, it is then possible to explain about bacteria and their various types, perhaps asking the students what kinds of parameters they would use to distinguish bacterial cell types. One should arrive, at least, at some minimal kind of classification of bacteria, perhaps just by shapes and sizes.

The term "molecule" could be taken up next perhaps just by a reminder of school chemistry and how the concept of molecule was arrived at. Then it is possible to ask about the major kinds of biologically important molecules. With some hints, the class will talk about proteins, sugars and starches, fats, and frequently in this day and age, nucleic acids which are, to them, genes or chromosomes and not, as I insist, acids found originally only in the nuclei. This may be a good point to appoint a class secretary by saying you would like to talk about how to establish the existence of such molecules and measure their separate concentrations, but there is no time. Therefore, ask a secretary to write down this question and to remind you of it some other day when the class work has been finished with some class time remaining. This strategy will give the class the secure feeling that all questions will eventually be answered.

Cultures and synthetic media can be discussed by raising the problem of how organisms obtain their raw materials. A culture medium must contain all the needed atomic species, but then there comes the problem of how these are formed into suitable larger molecules, and the instructor can in a very general way raise the question of biochemical strategy and energy.

Talking about molecules provides a good opportunity to go into the question of how to insert energy into a molecule. I usually do this by reminding students that, say, the oxygen molecule contains two atoms of oxygen. I draw these atoms on the blackboard some distance apart and ask students to indicate where the electrons and nuclei are. Then, it should be plausible that the atoms repel because the negative electrons are nearest each other. So, you have to push the atoms toward each other. This is similar to what happens when you compress a spring with two hands. I point out that if I let go when the atoms are still not very close together, they will fly apart, and I get work out of the system by hitching a string to the atoms and letting them pull something while they fly apart. Or, equally, we could let the separating atoms hit something after they have picked up speed and convert that impact into useful work, perhaps by operating a sort of ground-breaking hammer. Thus it is possible to indicate that potential energy is being stored as you do the work of pushing the (repelling) atoms together. Now the class will tell you that the atoms stick together to make a molecule when the atoms are very close together. Then, with hints, they will tell you that when the atoms get close enough, there must be a short-range force that begins to operate, otherwise there would never be a molecule. This short-range force I liken to a hook and eye, which I sketch on the board as holding a spring in compression after I have compressed it enough. The analogy usually lets students figure out how one can recover the stored energy. They indicate that giving the hook a little push will permit a large amount of stored energy to be released. The storage of energy in complex molecules is then an easy extrapolation for them. And, the recovery of the energy by taking the molecule apart is also not hard for them to develop. Thus, the catabolic and anabolic aspects of metabolism can be invented in the class room. In this way, it is possible to have the students raise many questions about fundamental biological attributes and to get them to think about how they themselves might go about determining the answers.

Having discussed all the terms associated with the first part of the paper (page 365, in this instance), the students can now be asked to explain the ideas of this part. This particular paper has the important advantage that there is explicit discussion of the problem of how to choose an organism for study of some biological question. Here, the experimental and methodological advantages of bacteriophages are explicitly listed. The authors then set forth the scope of the work they will present.

The next section for the students to study is the experimental part concerned with materials and methods. Among the many terms and ideas raised for discussion by the students will be Dr. Lindegren and his connection with the work, Difco nutrient broth, pH, growth factors, sewage filtrates, plaques, agar medium, exponential notation, lysates, sedimentation, filters, dilutions, assay value, inhibiting substances, polysaccharide fractions, plaque-counting method, phage-bacterium contact, sampling error, effect of bacterial concentration, temperature, Figure 1, and efficiency of plating. These are handled as was the first list of terms.

There are now opportunities for getting the students to think about how to measure things themselves. In addition, since data are presented, there is opportunity to ask why certain numbers are given. Why for example, is 100-1000 plaques called a "readily countable number"? Why is an 18-hour culture used? The question of why 6 to 24 hours of incubation was used can be taken up here or deferred (through the secretary) to a time after the latent period and burst size have been studied; in the latter instance, the reason for the definite size of the plaque is more readily discovered by the students. Why is 0.1 ml. used for spreading agar? In this connection it is desirable to bring into the classroom some of the tubes, pipettes, petri plates, etc. used in the work so that the students gain an idea of the items and sizes and liquid measures under discussion. 0.1 ml. will then have some meaning for them. Also, going through the mechanics of a dilution series will clarify much that is mysterious to most students.

Figure 1 is a very good first figure to study. The students can be asked how every number in the figure was ascertained, including the axes, because relative concentration is not at all understood by almost all students. Only when some student has really explained how at least two points in the figure were determined can the class be asked if all understand the source of the data. If the questions remain, the students can explain. Then, the data and their implications can be discussed. I always ask the students what alternative results might have been obtained, and what they would then have meant. I have, with suitably inclined students, spent an entire class hour on this figure, though most classes will not take such an intense examination of the figure so early in the course. At this point, just before boredom or restlessness sets in, it is of the greatest importance *for the instructor* to be aware of the fact that the information in the figure is not very important because the purpose and strategy of the course are to have the students learn what the biologist does and not the particular information in this figure or in this paper. That is, when the students become restless, the instructor must simply make a rough statement of what he thinks the students should learn from the figure and continue on to the next point. The students will eventually learn to read figures and tables, if they are not forced to learn it all on just one figure or table.

To prepare for studying the data of Table 1, it is useful to ask a student to go through the physical motions of making the dilutions in front of the class so as to discover by observation what factors could contribute to variability from plate to plate. If the instructor happens to know much about the statistical aspects of science, he can do a little bit on this part of the tables. If he happens not to know much, he should not raise the question. If the students raise the question he should set forth the way in which he himself considers the variations of data and then tell the students frankly that he doesn't feel competent to attempt a deeper explanation. One cannot teach what one doesn't *really* know, and students do much better with instructors who enhance their general credibility by not attempting to regurgitate scarcely grasped information whose flimsiness is readily guessed by students. For example, I can readily do the statistical aspects of data analysis, and students recognize this at once. They are equally adept at knowing they are being lectured at by an incompetent if I try to discuss very much about cell biochemistry beyond the molecular aspects.

We continue section by section. As each section is finished, the students are asked to imagine what the next work should be and then to find a way of justifying the title of the actual next section. What, for example, would they expect to find discussed under the heading of adsorption? Are there ways of knowing that phages have been adsorbed by sensitive bacteria? What ways? The students must imagine for themselves what is done to use a filter, and what comes through the filter; how much liquid and what is in it. If a centrifuge is used, what is done after the end of the centrifuging? What happens to the liquid supernatant fluid? What is in it? What other ways are there of measuring adsorption? Some student will always come up with the idea that one may be able selectively to kill bacteria, leaving free phages. The instructor can then help the students to imagine chemical (e.g. chloroform to lyse the cell), biological (antibiotics or antiserum), physical (sonication, grinding with glass beads) ways of doing this. Working on the problem of breaking cells apart will help the student develop the habit of thinking about how he would actually go about doing something with his own hands. The several ways should be listed on a blackboard. The instructor can then ask students to design ways of killing off the free phages. They will have some trouble, and if no one can make progress with this question, one can hint by asking students to look over the list of ways of killing the bacteria. Some student will usually propose a specific antiphage serum. Then, one can indicate that it is possible to measure total plaque-forming units, free phages, and infected bacteria, and that these must add up properly to give a check on the whole understanding.

Parenthetically, it is worth remarking here that this point can be returned to after the one-step growth curve has been analyzed, because one can get the students to consider the difference between a plaque formed by a free phage and one formed by an infected cell. Consideration of the dynamics of plaque formation, in whatever terms the instructor will present them, permits many students to assert that an infected cell will make a larger plaque than a free phage particle. Therefore, one can return to the one-step growth curve to ask what the plaques (in Figure 2) look like for the o-minute point, for the 5-, 10-, 20-, and 50 minute points. Most students are actually excited to realize that studying plaque size can tell them free phages from adsorbed phages so that they assert that the o-minute point has a variety of plaque diameters up to some upper limit, and that all the plaques are this largest or limit size on the 20-minute plate. A demonstration of plaques on a petri dish will crystallize all the understandings.

Why should multiple infection do anything? What kinds of things might be expected? Why might temperature be expected to affect anything? etc.

If the Poisson distribution is beyond the mathematical talent of the instructor, it should be skipped by admitting it. The students should be asked if they want the matter explained by some specialist. If they so desire, the instructor should arrange a carefully prepared *short* visit (15 minutes) by a competent colleague.

The Discussion should be read through carefully, preferably aloud by several students in turn. Each statement should be explained and then analyzed by the students. If any one point is not readily handled, it doesn't pay to hammer away at it.

In this particular paper, there is an explicit summary of very simple and direct nature. I have always found it useful to read each point aloud, and then go around the class asking gently if someone can indicate the experimental basis of each statement. If this is done well, the students gain the security of knowing that there is no penalty attached to not knowing something so that the classroom becomes a pressure-free place for trying to say things as you understand them, however dimly the light of understanding may be burning.

Lastly, the students should be asked to imagine what kinds of studies should be done next. With some hinting, they will in a half-hour come up with the idea of trying to measure the synthesis of the various macromolecules that make up phages, with trying to break open the infected cells at various times to measure their phage contents, and with the idea of looking with some kind of supermicroscope to see what is going on. With those suggestions, it is possible to announce that they next will read papers on just those suggested activities, and the first of these can be handed out. In my list, the next paper is one by S. S. Cohen on the synthesis of nucleic acid and protein in *Escherichia coli* infected with a coliphage.

Appendix 2

List of papers used for course on the DNA basis of heredity:

1. Emory L. Ellis and Max Delbrück. The growth of bacterio-phage. J. Gen. Physiol. 22, 365–384, 1939.
2. S. S. Cohen. The synthesis of bacterial viruses I. J. Biol. Chem. *174*, 281–293, 1948.
3. A. H. Doermann. The intracellular growth of bacteriophages. J. Gen. Physiol. *35*, 645–656, 1952.
4. A. D. Hershey and R. Rotman. Linkage among genes control-ling inhibition of lysis in a bacterial virus. Proc. Nat. Acad. Sci. *34*, 89–96, 1948.
5. A. D. Hershey and Martha Chase. Independent functions of viral protein and nucleic acid in growth of bacteriophage. J. Gen. Physiol. *36*, 39–56, 1952.
6. J. D. Watson and F. H. C. Crick. Genetical implications of the structure of deoxyribonucleic acid. Nature *171*, 964–969, 1953.
7. M. Meselson and J. J. Weigle. Chromosome breakage accom-panying genetic recombination in bacteriophage. Proc. Nat. Acad. Sci. *47*, 857–868, 1961.

Appendix 3
Student Comments

1. It gives the non-science oriented student an appreciation of the precision and complexity involved in scientific experimentation.
2. Actual experiments in a lab should be performed by students as a class to increase appreciation of scientific work.
3. It enables non-science majors to get to know how scientists operate, an important thing in this age.
4. Instead of learning a pre-determined amount of factual material, the particular material can be chosen by the group according to its interests and the evaluation of papers becomes interesting. This is the most meaningful type of course for the non-science major—it teaches him a skill which won't be forgotten.
5. This course allowed one to ask questions freely and expect answers without fear of showing ignorance. No regurgitation was expected. It can teach exactly what it purports to teach— the theory of science, not reams of trivia. It shows the layman that science is not necessarily exclusive to the professional scientist, in terms of interest and essential understanding.
6. This course can be extremely detrimental if taught by someone who is not interested in teaching it. It should not be an explanation section for various papers.

7. It is exactly a course with this kind of approach from which one can benefit the most. An approach like this does exactly what all college courses should do. I feel really thrilled that I can now pick up a scientific paper and have an idea about its content and be able to critically decide whether I feel it has any validity.

8. Learning by discussion and efforts to understand papers is so much nicer than learning by memorizing books and lecture notes. Reading and *understanding* scientific papers showed me science does not have to be such a mysterious, foreign world. (The) lack of emphasis on grades—no pressure—allowed for relaxed atmosphere.

9. The emphasis on analysis, thought, and criticism rather than memorization. Its encouragement of participation was excellent. I found it a most exciting and enjoyable experience. (However) one does need some general knowledge as background for reading research papers.

10. It gives one insight into the process through which scientific discoveries are made. It not only teaches one to view scientific papers with a degree of critical ability, but implements one's ability to read critically in general. It gives one appreciation for the many and varied problems that confront a scientist.

11. Learning is painless and you want to learn to find out why something happens or what comes next.

12. I think this course taught me to read and think critically and analytically, not to accept blindly everything that I read. After the semester was about ¾ over, the course became a bit redundant. I didn't feel that I was learning anything new.

13. This course causes the students to think creatively and scientifically. There is no pressure or emphasis on grades; this makes (it) more conducive for students to learn for learning's sake.

14. The method of learning—exploring one particular field of science just as the scientist would—was valuable not only in understanding the field of science, but in understanding the problems the scientist faced then and actually faces today. I never enjoyed a science course until this year.

15. By allowing the instructors to use papers in their fields, it made the course very exciting. A knowledge of the subject was not necessary. The purpose (I believe) was to show how a scientist goes about his work. I have come out of this course with an understanding of both the approach and the material.

16. In doing away with rote memorization and other trivia, it managed to hold the interest of a non-scientist like me—and, in holding my interest so completely, it enabled me to learn stuff which before I would have dismissed as "too boring" or "too complex" to even try to absorb. It succeeded in making bio a "why" or "how" course, not simply a "what" course. Thanks for the first biology course . . . in which I think I really learned something that I'll retain past the final exam.

17. There is almost no pressure on the student while taking the course. He may be creative or not as he chooses. I particularly enjoyed the freedom of thought allowed in this class. The use of real experimental results . . . was also good. The major defect is . . . that no matter how well this course is taught, one cannot keep studying the same material (with a few variations) for 4 months.

18. The exams, test, etc. are teaching you to think instead of recall. Not enough basic interest in science among students to really apply ourselves in class. If given the course again, I would think and participate more actively.

19. I had never wanted to take Bio. Sci., but I found the classes often exciting—especially when we were devising experiments or developing theories about a biological process.

20. By choosing a very specific topic and going into the subject in depth, explaining all the basic material involved and studying the experiments of scientists, the student gains an understanding of scientific approaches to research and appreciates the fact that he can *comprehend* the material instead of dogmatically memorizing it! I wish we could have spent a little more time relating the findings . . . to actual applications. I liked having take home exams, but one of these—an unlimited time exam—I found overwhelming and I worked on it for *13* hours! I think it is preferable to set a time limit.

21. The course proceeds at the rate of those in it. The classes are small enough so that interest can be stimulated and continued by a knowledgeable prof. If all students become open, no one should be left behind. I feel I learned a lot about the approach in general and the topics covered.

22. Without great pressure I feel I have acquired a basic knowledge of the material covered in class. The classroom situation was very informal and I found it easy to ask any questions I had. I found that when the instructor asked us to write down any questions, we had much more participation in the next class period.

23. The course teaches a way of approaching problems and solving them, and gives the non-science major an insight into the challenges of the sciences. Instead of burdening us with a lot of detailed information that we'd never have any use for, we studied one subject with the object of understanding it.

24. The course provides an opportunity to study the biologist's approach to biology rather than requiring the student to memorize minute details which he'd forget the day after the final. Now the students should be able to approach a biological problem with some knowledge of the proper scientific tools.

25. Intimacy of class, ability to witness closely the enthusiasm and personality of a biologist eager to teach and contagious in her desire for us to learn. Assignments *sort of* easy—able to salvage your ignorance fortunately. Too damned hard materials —enormously sophisticated papers, at least for me. She asked us to ask questions, but after a while I couldn't—my fault probably. Grading not stiff, a plus for senior English majors like me.

26. The student finally learns what biology is and what a biologist does, what techniques he uses in research. It gives a glimpse into the problems and potential a biologist works with. The student, without memorizing or knowing a lot of biology, can reason out problems and devise his own experiments if the instructor is challenging in his presentation.

27. Even though we were covering complicated material, there was a genuine effort made to make everyone feel at ease so that

everyone felt relaxed enough to ask questions about what they didn't understand.

28. The relatively unstructured nature of the direction taken as a result of the experiments. That is, after orderly discussion of an experiment . . . the class can utilize the expertise of the professor to explore areas OF INTEREST TO THE STUDENTS. In a friendly, relaxed manner . . . Dr. X encouraged the interest of many students previously "turned off" by science. As a non-science major, I enjoyed this course, much to my surprise.

29. It captured the interest even of a person who has previously met failure after failure in attempting to understand and enjoy science.

30. The most important knowledge regarding the sciences for a non-science major is understanding of procedure and approach rather than idiosyncratic facts. The basic theories, or way of constructing and proving theories presented in this course are relevant to many non-science fields . . . I occasionally felt that the professor would make her knowledge of a certain scientific area appear more complete than it actually was.

31. It doesn't jam facts down your throat that you will forget 10 minutes after a test. Even though you learn a very limited topic, what you do learn stays with you because of the way you accumulated your knowledge. My chief complaint was that the subject matter was really irrelevant to me. I know that phage studies have parallel functions in man, but it took more than $\frac{2}{3}$ of the semester to realize this.

32. I enjoyed knowing Dr. X, but I found the course to be usually above my level of comprehension and therefore I lost interest.

33. It encourages the students to ask questions and distinguish between a random questioning and a scientific method of asking the proper questions.

34. The method, philosophy, and technique are more than competent. But, the subject matter has too little relevance to draw the same enthusiasm as the instructor's.

35. I believe that for a person in the social sciences, like myself,

it is able to give him an appreciation of the scientific method. I also got a feel for the excitement in the world of people doing biology. The question format helped me to formulate questions in my own mind about what I did not understand.

36. The course was interesting because students could ask almost any question without feeling stupid (that is, if the teacher didn't intimidate them). Also, the pace of the material studied was set by the students. This lack of pressure led to getting interested in the material.

37. The course teaches you to think rather than to memorize much scientific material. Also, it makes you aware of how a scientist thinks, how he must sort out this material, etc. Finally, I think the course makes science less formidable for non-science majors. I think our final exam was not up to the level of the course. I would have preferred either a take-home or else an exam that required imagination—certainly not an exam that required outlining.

38. It gave the opportunity for students to see the workings of a scientist—his task, his difficulties, his conclusions. It helps for a better understanding of the scientific process.

39. A better understanding of the scientific method than would be true in a lecture-memorization course. The method is something that will be retained and used in one's everyday reading material. This approach promotes class discussion.

40. Getting away from broad generalities to learning one microfield in depth.

41. The new approach to this course was really great, the idea that you read a paper you've never seen before and after a few days, it's just like you're the scientist. I really liked this course because it didn't matter what you already knew; it was a question of did you get anything out of the scientific research paper you read.

42. The material was much too deep, dull, and uninteresting. It was all right while it lasted.

43. One is not forced to memorize a lot of petty facts but rather to try to learn to follow other people's line of thinking and to think things through for oneself. I found the reading for the

course much, much, much too difficult. I think that the basic idea behind a course of this nature is good, but in this specific instance, I positively hated it. I see no reason why we couldn't have started out reading somewhat easier papers and worked our way up to more difficult ones. Some of us never recovered from the initial shock.

44. Minimum amount of work for maximum benefit. Insights into modern scientific problems, science's social responsibilities. There should be more research papers relevant to problems concerning non-science majors.

45. That for people like me who are not especially interested in biology, it can arouse interest and be an enjoyable way to learn about some aspects of scientific approaches.

46. It is interesting for non-science majors. It also helps in relating to other courses, in knowing how to look at a problem.

47. The course was interesting; it helped give a better idea of how scientists think and approach problems. Reading the actual scientific literature helped overcome the idea that scientific articles are magical but can be understood, given some persistence, a dictionary, and background.

DATE DUE

'93